AN OPERA
IN 3 ACTS
STARRING
GINO QUILICO

.ll.

AN OPERA IN 3 ACTS

STARRING GINO QUILICO

a biography

CONNIE GUZZO-MCPARLAND

.ll.

This book is a work of creative non-fiction. It is based on the actual events of the lives and careers of Lina, Louis, and Gino Quilico. Though remaining true to the facts as represented in interviews with various family members, the author has taken some creative licence in dramatizing some scenes and imagining dialogue.

Prepared for the press by: Jennifer McMorran
Cover design: Leila Marshy, Debbie Geltner
Cover image: Gino Quilico as Don Giovanni, Toronto, 1988, Robert Cahen Photography
Author photo: Yvette Capko Photographs

Unless otherwise identified, all photographs appear in these pages courtesy the Quilico family. While every effort has been made to secure the sources and permissions for the photographic materials contained in this book, we would welcome further assistance regarding crediting these materials. In future editions, we will readily acknowledge further sources and permissions.

Library and Archives Canada Cataloguing in Publication

Title: An opera in 3 acts, starring Gino Quilico / Connie Guzzo-McParland
Other titles: Opera in three acts, starring Gino Quilico
Names: Guzzo-McParland, Connie, 1947- author.
Identifiers: Canadiana (print) 2022019100X | Canadiana (ebook) 20220191069 | ISBN 9781773901244 (softcover) | ISBN 9781773901251 (EPUB) | ISBN 9781773901268 (PDF)
Subjects: LCSH: Quilico, Gino. | LCSH: Quilico, Louis—Family. | LCSH: Singers—Canada—Biography.
Classification: LCC ML420 .Q55 G99 2022 | DDC 782.1092—dc23

Printed and bound in Canada.

The publisher gratefully acknowledges the support of the Government of Canada through the Canada Council for the Arts, the Canada Book Fund, and of the Government of Quebec through
the Société de développement des entreprises culturelles (SODEC) and the Programme de credit d'impôt pour l'édition de livres—Gestion SODEC.

Linda Leith Éditions
Montreal
www.lindaleith.com

To my late father, Antonio, and my brother Vincenzo—who loved opera—but, because of their untimely deaths, never attained their dream of attending a performance at La Scala.

Contents

A Note from the Author

I have always been fascinated by the stories of talented and accomplished people and I'm especially drawn to the world of music. I grew up in a music- and opera-loving family. My earliest memory of my father is of him singing *"Una furtiva lacrima..."* with a dramatically sad face and teary eyes, while stirring tomato sauce on Sunday mornings.

He was an amateur musician. In Italy, he played trumpet in a village band, and after emigrating to Montreal, he joined a similar band that played at Italian religious processions. For a short period, he and a friend formed an orchestra that played at weddings, and he practised on his trumpet almost every day. My brother Vincenzo studied music and the same instrument seriously, first with my father, later with Professor Massimo Rossi of Montreal, and then with top professional musicians of the instrument. Being a practical person, he never attempted to make a career from music, but music did govern his life, and he spent an inordinate amount of time on his trumpet exercises and studies. He also directed several church choirs and organized concerts, primarily for fundraising. Without any expectation of making money as a musician, he was happy to perform with classical singers and other musicians.

In the spring of 2000, Vincenzo organized a successful fundraising concert at the Mount Carmel Church, in suburban Saint-Léonard with a world-renowned special guest, the baritone Louis Quilico, who was known as Mr. Rigoletto. Vincenzo had a great sense of accomplishment and happiness at the end of that evening and was especially impressed by the famous baritone's generosity and friendliness. Sadly, however, that concert turned out to be his last, and Louis Quilico, died the following July.

Vincenzo made the acquaintance of Gino Quilico a few years later. Together with friends Michelle Hekimi and Ginette Solomon, both classical singers, my brother founded the Voices of Hope choir with cancer patients of the Jewish General Hospital of Montreal, and Gino sang at one of their fundraising concerts.

A comical situation developed a few minutes before the start of the show when Gino was changing into his tuxedo and realized that he had forgotten his white shirt. Vincenzo paced nervously, wondering if he should give up his own shirt, or have Gino go on stage with just a T-shirt under his tuxedo. Gino, unfazed, simply asked if there was a clothing store nearby. They announced a delay to the start of the concert due to a last-minute technical problem, while Gino went shopping nearby. The owner of Boutique Jacques refused payment after recognizing Gino and hearing the concert was a fundraiser. Not only did Gino return with the right shirt, but he made everyone laugh when he told the audience the real reason for the delay and of the boutique owner's generosity. This was the first time I had met Gino and I was charmed as much by his singing as by his fun-loving nature.

A friendship developed between my brother and Gino that lasted until my brother's premature death in 2015. A few months before Vincenzo took ill, he had played at Gino's *Serata D'Amore* concert. Gino often came to visit Vincenzo in hospital and sang at his funeral.

After publishing two works of fiction, I was eager to tackle a work of non-fiction. I began searching for subjects with a Montreal connection. I considered a number of well-known personalities and families, but before contacting any of them, one family stood out for me, and that was, of course, the Quilico Family. I knew little about the details of their lives, except that Louis and Gino Quilico had achieved world-renowned fame and that Lina Pizzolongo, wife and mother of the two baritones, had contributed to their careers. I also realized that, like me, many Montrealers outside of the music world were not aware of the calibre of this family's talent and the story behind their struggle to achieve world fame.

I reached out to Gino and asked for his collaboration. He graciously agreed to be interviewed and has been very forthcoming with background information. It took only one meeting for me to realize the love and appreciation he felt for his mother, Lina. In my efforts to find a unique voice and tone for the book, it came to me that the most fitting person to recount the story of the family would be Lina. I never met her, but I heard Lina's strong and powerful voice in Gino's retelling of their story. I was able to channel Lina and imagine her speaking to herself and to all of us. After taking that creative license, it was easy to do the same for Louis and Gino and thus the idea of three voices in three acts became the stage upon which the story would be set. Many of the words are taken directly from my interviews with Gino; some I have paraphrased from other sources, some I've put into their mouths. At all times, I have striven to be faithful to how their story unfolded and to preserve the integrity of their personalities.

Though I aimed to chronicle the facts and events of the rise of the Quilico family from humble beginnings in east-end Montreal to fame at the New York Met, the Paris Opera, La Scala and other great opera houses, how Lina and Louis have told their story from beyond is very much a fictionalized account.

I have juxtaposed the creative narrative with some actual photos and quotes from reviews and articles written at different periods of their careers. These add factual details and tell their own story.

Lastly, I did not conceive this biography as an exposition or dissertation on music, voice technique, the art of opera, or the operatic arts scene. My focus lay with the personal and human emotions behind the makeup, the elaborate costumes, and the masks worn by its protagonists, Gino Quilico and his family. As Gino provided the most first-hand information, the focus of the book falls on him.

As I moved forward with the project, it became apparent that what drew me to their story was the admiration and appreciation I feel for those who dedicate their lives to bringing music and beauty to the world. The Quilico family has achieved this human triumph three times over.

Connie Guzzo-McParland
April 2022

Endorsements

When I first met Gino Quilico, I was an assistant conductor at the Metropolitan Opera in the late 1980s. Gino Quilico was already known as the "Wünderkind young baritone," considered to be the finest of his young generation. He had already had an extensive recording career and had worked with the great opera superstars of our time, such as Luciano Pavarotti and Mirella Freni. Gino, ever energetic, with a quick wit, good looks and endearing charisma, was a fan favourite and a pleasure for his musical colleagues. Making matters even more interesting was that he was the son of the great opera star Louis Quilico, one of the most celebrated Verdi baritones in the world, and considered to be a national treasure in Canada.

This Italo-Canadian family, which I used to call, "The Quilico Dynasty," was held together and run by his mother, Lina. I was fortunate enough as a young conductor, to have collaborated with Louis Quilico in one of his favourite charitable projects, "Water for Africa," held yearly in Toronto, Canada. The first years I participated in this, Lina was still alive and I witnessed first-hand that she, being an excellent pianist and coach, was the true power behind the throne. Like a true drill sergeant, she coached and taught her husband Louis and her son, Gino, to be prepared for their operatic roles on every level. It was a great pleasure conducting father/son duets—on these early charitable concerts.

Gino and I experienced our first of many wonderful collaborations working on the Metropolitan Opera's world premiere of John

Corigliano's "The Ghosts of Versailles." Gino made an impossibly difficult role seem exciting and fun and the set bar ever higher for anyone attempting to tackle the role in the future. This was the first of many entertaining musical adventures together that resulting in not only a working relationship but a true friendship as well. From Tchaikovsky's "Eugene Onegin" in Philadelphia to Mozart's, "Don Giovanni" in Detroit and even several concerts at the St. Barth's Festival in later years, Gino has always been a generous colleague and a joy with whom to make music. Over the years, he has proven himself to be an exceptionally versatile artist singing opera, Neapolitan songs and Broadway repertoire.

Ultimately, he has done his family proud by carrying the Louis/Lina Quilico Musical Legacy forward as both a modern day teacher and stage director. I've considered myself one of the fortunate few who can say they have experienced both mother, father and son in a musical light-the whole Quilico Dynasty. It has been an honour and a privilege.

Maestro Steven Mercurio
March 2022

I was fortunate enough in my musical endeavors to work with the Quilicos, both, father and son, and I can only underline that I had the greatest pleasure to make music with these great artists. If it was *Otello* with Louis or *Les Troyens & Carmen* with Gino, their amazing talent will remain unforgettable to me.

In admiration and respect,

Maestro Zubin Mehta
June 2021

Prelude
Milan, 1991

Opera is as much of an addiction as any drug. Its dealers and pushers, otherwise known as impresarios, see to it that dependence for the grandiose art form that had its glory days in Baroque Italy is perpetuated, whether in its original form or its many modern and post-modern permutations. For spectators with a flair for extravagant melodrama, the fix comes in the form of finely packaged great music, glorious voices, live theatre, beautiful ballet, grand stage settings. Professionally trained performers like me, gifted with a strong voice box, are first lured in by the dream of fame, then the grand spectacle of it all keeps us hooked, to say nothing of the high derived from applause and standing ovations that keep one wanting more. Once pulled into that world, you need a big ego and a thick skin to survive its rigid demands and the high price extracted by the elusive search for glory. I've developed both over the years, but today, I feel the urge to say, "*Basta!*"

I'm in Milan, inside its famous cathedral, the Duomo, a few metres away from the Teatro alla Scala, the most venerated opera house in the world. Verdi, Puccini, Rossini have conducted their masterpieces here to adoring fans and to some catcalls, too. The audience at La Scala is the most demanding, they say!

On my way to the church, I paused in front of the theatre to look at the simple marquee framed by the Red Cross and Crown emblem of the

TEATRO ALLA SCALA

STAGIONE D'OPERA E BALLETTO 1990/91
(40ª dalla fondazione del Teatro)

Rappr. N. 152

Turno C

MARTEDÌ 4 GIUGNO 1991 · ORE 20
PRIMA RAPPRESENTAZIONE

LA BOHÈME

Quattro quadri - Libretto di GIUSEPPE GIACOSA e LUIGI ILLICA
(dalle "Scènes de la vie de bohème" di Henri Murger)

Musica di

GIACOMO PUCCINI

(Proprietà G. Ricordi & C., S.p.A., Milano)

Personaggi	Interpreti
Rodolfo	RICHARD LEECH
Schaunard	STEFANO ANTONUCCI
Benoit	CLAUDIO GIOMBI
Mimì	MIRELLA FRENI
Marcello	GINO QUILICO
Colline	GIORGIO SURJAN
Alcindoro	ENZO CAPUANO
Musetta	DENIA MAZZOLA
Parpignol	ERNESTO GAVAZZI
Sergente dei doganieri	ALDO BRAMANTE
Un doganiere	ERNESTO PANARIELLO
Un venditore	LUIGI COLNAGHI

Concertatore e direttore d'orchestra
GIANANDREA GAVAZZENI

Direttore del coro
ROBERTO GABBIANI

Regia e scene di
FRANCO ZEFFIRELLI

Costumi di
MARCEL ESCOFFIER

Direttore delle luci
GIANNI MANTOVANINI

Direttore dell'allestimento scenico
RAOUL FAROLFI

Direttore musicale del palcoscenico
CARLO CAMERINI

Regista stabile e direttore della produzione
ANTONELLO MADAU DIAZ

Maestro collaboratore di sala
GABRIELE PISANI

Aiuto regista
MARINA BIANCHI

Maestro rammentatore
DANTE MAZZOLA

Direttore di scena
PAOLO TOMASELLI

Altri maestri di sala
ARNOLD BOSMAN   MAURIZIO MAGNI

Maestri collaboratori di palcoscenico
MASSIMILIANO BULLO   LUCA DE PERINI   MASSIMO GUANTINI   GIUSEPPE MORASCHI

Altro maestro del coro
BRUNO CASONI

Pittori scenografi realizzatori
MARIO MANTOVANI   ANTONIO MOLINARI   GINO ROMEI   ANGELO SALA

Maestro alle luci
PAOLO ARATA

Responsabile archivio musicale
CARLO TABARELLI

Capo servizio laboratori
ANACLETO CHIODI

Capo reparto macchinisti
MICHELE MERCURIO

Vice capo reparto macchinisti
ANTONIO MERCURIO

Capo reparto sartoria
CINZIA ROSSELLI

Capo reparto elettricisti
SALVATORE MANCINELLI

Capo reparto costruzioni
SANTE FACCI

Capo reparto attrezzisti
LUIGI METALDI

Capo reparto meccanici
GIANCARLO ASTORRI

L'OPERA SI RAPPRESENTA IN TRE PARTI, CON INTERVALLI DOPO IL SECONDO E DOPO IL TERZO ATTO

Si ringrazia per la collaborazione

GRUPPO
Eni

PREZZI (Tasse comprese)

Poltrona di platea L. 200.000 · Poltroncina di platea L. 160.000
Posto in palco L. 160.000 · Ingresso supplementare ai palchi L. 80.000
Prima galleria: poltroncina L. 50.000 · numerato L. 38.000 · ingresso L. 5.000
Seconda galleria: poltroncina L. 40.000 · numerato L. 20.000 · ingresso L. 5.000

Sui biglietti dei posti riservati o acquistati nei giorni precedenti quello dello spettacolo si applica il 10% di servizio prenotazione.
A termine di legge è vietato, durante lo spettacolo, effettuare anche parzialmente, riprese filmate o registrazioni e scattare fotografie in sala o nei ridotti.

Gino Quilico
Debut

Teatro alla Scala. It announces the *prima rappresentazione* of *La Bohème*, by Giacomo Puccini, conducted by Maestro Gianandrea Gavazzeni, and directed by the famous movie director, Franco Zeffirelli, with tenor Richard Leech as Rodolfo, Mirella Freni as Mimi, Gino Quilico as Marcello. That's me, Gino, playing Marcello, one of my favourite roles.

I've come to the cathedral every day after rehearsals to light a candle for my mother, who is not well and could not be here for one of my most important debuts. My heart broke when she stayed home in bed when I left to realize her dream of bringing at least one Quilico to perform at La Scala. My pinnacle moment of success felt empty without her by my side. Would it be real if she could not see me, hear me? I've suffered from these thoughts the entire month, going through the motions of rehearsing with an insufferable conductor who takes himself for a god and belittles me at every opportunity. Today, after his last tirade against me, ever gracious Mirella Freni took me aside and said, *"Non ne vale la pena."* It's not worth getting angry over him. I escaped to the cathedral to pray and soothe my aching heart.

I've lingered inside here longer than usual, wishing I had feigned illness and walked out of the production when I had the chance. This is not my first debut, and I'm used to performance-night jitters, but the apprehension I feel now is different. It's not the panic of failure, but more like an ominous fear hovering over me like a dark shadow—a fear that the years of study, travel, living in hotels have me deluded. All this—and now Maestro Gavazzeni? I knew his reputation as an egocentric director. In spite of my full schedule at the Paris Opera, where I don't have to put up with arrogant conductors, I was elated to be invited to sing at La Scala. Franco Zeffirelli's reputation as a movie director is nothing to sneeze at, for one thing. And I wanted to make my mother happy.

"La Scala is still La Scala, no matter what! At least one Quilico must sing there," she said.

The only time I've walked out of a performance was in Cincinnati at the very beginning of my career. I holed up in a cheap hotel for two weeks, fighting imaginary demons, before I resumed singing. That caprice cost me dearly professionally.

I do believe in signs. On the day I met Maestro Gavazzeni, he reminded me of the mental anguish I'd suffered in that distant past. His outbursts and our mutual antipathy felt like the portent of bad things to come.

I speak to my mother daily and have told her about some some of my spats with the maestro. "Do as you please," she told me. "The Quilicos have proven themselves on the world stage and don't need the approval of this maestro anymore, but just don't be a *divo*! What would Marcello do?"

In the dim and cool quietness of the cavernous cathedral, with rays of sun filtering through the stained-glass windows and the noises of the city muffled, I try to find an answer to her question. She has groomed and coached me for this role as for every other. I hear her voice in my ears with every breath I take on stage. It's early morning in Toronto, and I know she has planned to follow my performance from her bed, listening to the recording. I sense her presence.

ACT I

Lina and the Bohemians

Chapter 1
Toronto, 1991

I always knew he'd make the perfect Marcello—artistic, fun-loving, impetuous, cocky, but gentle with a heart as big as his voice, a voice as big as his ego. Tonight, he's debuting at La Scala as Gino Quilico—my son and star pupil. Only I'm not with him. I've been indisposed for a few months now, but my spirit is hovering over him, and he knows it. He has lit a candle at the Duomo for me every day since he arrived in Milano.

This is the first debut of his that I'm not attending in person. When he flew in from Paris, he had the cab stop at the Duomo even though he was late for the first rehearsal. I had warned him it was not a good idea to be late to his first meeting with an Italian conductor, and especially not Maestro Gavazzeni, but Gino can be cheeky when he senses arrogance.

When he got to the theatre, the maestro glared at him coldly— enough, Gino said, "to freeze a glass of Prosecco on a hot Italian July day." Rather than excuse himself and explain he'd had no choice but to take the morning flight from Paris because of his performance the night before, he joked that he thought they'd be working on Italian flex time.

The Maestro snapped back, "No special privileges for American recording stars."

I implored Gino to be respectful, if only because of the maestro's age and stellar reputation. He has conducted every great opera singer, including La Callas, at La Scala since the 1940s, and I suspect that they had just gotten off on the wrong foot. I've read that Gavazzeni does not subscribe to the star system of singers and conductors, and he has judged some experimental directorial choices as "presumptuous recklessness— to the detriment of musical performance." I've heard, too, that he dislikes recordings of operas. Gino has recorded over a dozen operas so far and has seven videos and two films under his belt, including *La Bohème*, directed by the much-respected Luigi Comencini.

Gino's late grand entrance had clearly rubbed Gavazzeni the wrong way. And Gino remembered he had promised me he'd play by the rules. "*Scusa, Maestro*," he said, bowing in his most affected baroque manner.

I've been coaching my son since the start of his career, and I've never tried to curb his tendency to stand up for himself. I've firmly redirected any impulse for pomposity into the vigour required to sing as a baritone. Neither father nor son has disappointed me in this regard, though the son does tend to push pompous conductors' buttons.

Oh, the excitement and the thrill of an opening! I've lived it so many times with Louis, who will be at the tonight's debut, though Gino doesn't know it yet. Louis has played in all the great opera houses but never at La Scala. If he's a little jealous, he certainly hasn't shown it. We all know it's Louis, more than any other person, who inspired Gino to pursue his dream of singing opera. And it's Louis who gifted Gino with a great voice, without which neither father nor son would have made it. Gino's debut tonight is a dream come true for all of us and especially meaningful for Louis, whose grandfather left Italy as an immigrant, and whose father ran a bicycle store in Montreal. They would never have dreamed of such an honour.

Gino's career is just now starting to peak. He has already achieved much, but he's still very young. I always believed he would make it, though there were many moments when he seemed to be going against the grain. I did everything I could to make him believe in himself as I had succeeded in making Louis believe in his own rare talent.

Maestro Gavazzeni not only seems to lack a sense of humour, but he has been reprimanding Gino unduly for the slightest mistaken gesture. He certainly can't pick on his singing, for Gino knows Marcello's role inside out. It's not one of the most musically challenging roles for a baritone and does not require the same intensity as Figaro or Don Giovanni, but it's one of the roles he enjoys most and one of the easiest for him to sing. "This Maestro thinks he's Italy's gift to the entire music world," he complained, "and he's treating me like a schoolboy."

The last straw was that the Maestro referred to him as the "*Americano*" rather than by his name. That struck a nerve.

"I'm glad *he* knows my identity! For years, even I didn't know whether to consider myself an American, a Canadian, or an Italian."

At the last rehearsals, Gino wore a woollen scarf, feigning a sore throat. His tentative plan was to walk out on the production, and, as he added, "Have my pipsqueak understudy sing the part unprepared—and have the great Maestro look like the *merde* that he is!"

He asked for my permission to walk out, and for once, I told him to do as he pleased, but I did ask him reflect on the time that he has invested preparing for this performance and the consequences of burning his bridges at La Scala. And I did suggest he not to be petty.

"What would Marcello do?" I asked him. I know Gino immerses himself in his roles completely, so I'm sure he'll think and act like a Marcello.

It would of course disappoint me if La Scala didn't happen, but this spat and Gino's reaction to it has me worried for other reasons. Behind the swagger, Gino is sensitive to negativity. The strongest egos can also be the most fragile! Unknown to Gino, I sent Louis to be present at the opening, just in case.

I'm not worried about the bad publicity that would follow, but only about my son's state of mind in the aftermath of such a drastic decision. From where I sit now, the tantrums of self-absorbed maestros seem so petty. On the other hand, Gino Quilico has made it to La Scala, and if he should leave of his own volition, I'll respect his choice. But I asked him to call me if he decides not to go on. His father has often stood up to maestros, but he's never walked out on one yet.

I must confess, though, that the thought of this debut has kept my morale up for months. I've felt as excited as I was for Louis's first important openings—and I'm now anxious about whether it will happen at all!

I know that Gino was heartbroken that I couldn't be present in person, but I told him to pretend I'm sitting on the balcony across from the stage. In reality, I'm lying on my bed in Toronto and listening to his recording of *La Bohème*. Isn't pretending what we artists do best?

I'll be watching as from above, not as a backstage coach, but as the spectator of an opera performance that, more than any other, mirrors our family's life—the life that is opera. I'll close my eyes and let life take its course. I will trick myself into believing that I, Lina Pizzolongo, pianist and voice coach, am entering La Scala, taking in the sounds, lights, and colours of the first-night performance of Puccini's *La Bohème*.

After a concert at La Scala, the French writer Stendhal wrote, "I believe La Scala is the premier theatre worldwide because it brings the most intense musical pleasure."

I pretend to be lingering outside the theatre like any other spectator. When the doors open, statues of Donizetti, Rossini, Puccini, Verdi, and other great Italian composers greet me in the lobby. A dazzling chandelier and guilt columns transport me to another era and way of life, when opera was the most anticipated musical happening of the season and composers the pop stars of the day. I can almost hear the sounds of the horse-drawn carriages delivering ladies in gowns and gentlemen in capes over black smoking jackets.

La Scala has a dress code, but that's for tourists, who are easily spotted. In North America, we have democratized opera. From every walk of life, opera lovers can afford to attend a performance in modern concert halls dressed casually. Italians don't need a dress code; they instinctively have a sense of pomp and circumstance and so dress appropriately: women in silks, beads, *paillettes*, and men in black. Italians take a night at the opera seriously, if only as an opportunity to wear their finest evening wear.

The *platea* is a sea of plush red velvet, surrounded by the highly decorated guilt balconies, with a large central loge built for royalty and nobility. As people trickle in, musicians start tuning their instruments, beginning with a few wind instruments, followed by strings until there's a cacophony of sounds that mix and mingle with the chattering of patrons.

The audience likes to linger, to see and be seen in the lobby, so the theatre remains empty until the lights turn on and off to advise the spectators to take their seats. The auditorium can accommodate more than 2000 people. With the balconies overflowing with finely dressed music lovers, the U-shaped structure of the theatre exudes even more electricity and splendour than the chandeliers and gilt-painted walls. It's the charge of high expectations!

It's 8 p.m. in Milan. The lights go out; the orchestra pit lights up. Not everyone pays attention to the orchestra pit, but I'm a musician, and

Puccini's operas are as much about the beauty of the music as the beauty of the voices. The two elements marry beautifully in his art.

The imaginary seat I prefer is in a balcony so that I can best observe the stage, the orchestra pit, the public sitting on the *platea,* and the thousand expectant faces of those in the other balconies. Let us not forget the *leggionisti* on the uppermost level. I see it all in my head.

Maestro Gavazzeni makes his appearance to the applause of the audience. The first note strikes; all eyes and ears are on the stage. The red and gold curtains open to a scene designed by Franco Zeffirelli that takes the audience to an artist's sparsely furnished garret in 1930 Paris.

An easel with a half-finished canvas of a sea is the focal point, and books are everywhere. It's winter, cold outdoors and indoors. Rodolfo looks out the window at the snow-covered roofs.

Is Marcello, my Marcello, on stage?

My phone has remained silent, so I need not have worried. I imagine Gino/Marcello lighting up the stage as he sings, *"Questo Mar Rosso* mi ammollisce, e assidera come se addosso mi piovesse in stille." The Red Sea staring at him from the canvas makes him feel numb.

Gino is singing at La Scala! Of that, I'm certain. I imagine his self-assured gestures. The music and the first scene sparkle with joie de vivre, though the artists are cold and hungry. The poet, Rodolfo, and the painter, Marcello, are the struggling artists, what the French called bohemians after the Roma who had fled to France from Bohemia. Their youth, their love affairs, and their love of art matter more to them than the squalid conditions of their lives.

Marcello sums up his first major piece of the evening as he blows on his hands to warm up, *"Ho un freddo cane."*

I shiver to think of the hand-to-mouth existence of struggling artists. As I listen to Puccini's score, a host of characters from my family's past drift in and out of my consciousness until they become one with Marcello, Rodolfo, Mimi....

Chapter 2
The Early Years - 1930s

My life unfolds in scenes as if on stage, as I follow the opera from my bed.

We lived on Drolet Street in Mile End, a working-class district of Montreal. I remember outdoor metal staircases, icy in winter, that were typical of houses in that part of town—how mother cursed them! We never thought of ourselves as poor, though my mother's idea of wealth was to live in a home that had an indoor flight of stairs.

My mother and I were walking home from school in the late afternoon. There was a biting wind and no sun to brighten up the snow that had fallen since morning. Mother pulled me by the hand as I ran to keep up with her hurried pace.

The snow had come early, and Mother had scampered to find gloves and a tuque to send my sister Irene and me off to school in. I had to wear my sister's old fall coat while she wore the new one Mother had bought for her at Morgan's.

"The delivery truck is coming and won't find anyone home," Mother said.

"What are they bringing?"

"A surprise for Irene."

Irene had her music lesson after school and would be home later. She was three years older than me and walked home by herself.

It must be a big surprise, I thought, if they needed a truck to deliver it. Irene always got the best surprises. I was cold and jealous. We had walked from school on Dante Street, along Bélanger, and then on Drolet, and as we crossed Jean-Talon to our building, on the corner, I could see a big truck outside our house and two burly men pacing at the staircase.

"Jeez, your father is late, too!"

Mother waved and ran towards the men. They jumped into the truck as we climbed upstairs and Mother opened the door. I watched them drag out a massive piece of furniture covered in blankets. It had legs, looked like a narrow table. What was Irene going to do with a table?

They rested it on the sidewalk and moved back to the truck, as if to drive away. Mother yelled at them from the top of the stairs.

« *Messieurs, ou allez-vous? Qui va le transporter en haut ?* »
« *Pas nous, sacrifice! Cette calice d'escalier est bien trop glissante et dangereuse* ! »

Mother argued with them, and they kept on cursing the slippery staircase. I covered my ears and ran inside to get away from the wind and the angry men. They could have left the table on the street for all I cared.

I soon heard my father's calm voice, telling the men what to do. He worked as a marble cutter and was used to handling heavy pieces of marble—fireplace mantels, columns, boxes of tiles—and carrying them in to people's homes. We had lived in that house for as long as I could remember, and I'd seen him manoeuvre heavy objects up the narrow spiral staircase. He patiently directed the two men upstairs with the heavy table, and they finally plunked it inside the apartment. Father offered them a beer. They seemed surprised or embarrassed by the offer, refused, and asked him to sign a paper. They pulled the blanket off the table before they left, and an upright piano appeared in the centre of our double living room as if by magic.

I couldn't contain my joy at the sight of the piano, our own piano, like the one we had at school. "Is it all for Irene?" I asked. "Are we keeping it?"

"It's all ours," Father said. "Archambault will let me pay in instalments. Irene can now take lessons at home, with Mlle Hubert." Father loved music and singing and all things artistic. Irene was the one he wanted to realize his dream of a musical career, and Mlle Hubert was the best piano teacher in town.

"I hope she'll let me touch it," I said.

"Maybe when you're older."

I needn't have feared. Though Irene's face also lit up when she saw the piano, she wasn't as protective of it as she had been of her dolls. A few days after the delivery, Mlle Hubert started coming in once a week for the lessons. Irene practised dutifully, but not as enthusiastically as Father had hoped. I was in the same room, pretending to do my homework, but paying attention of Mlle Hubert's instructions. I watched Mlle Hubert's nimble hands run over the keys. How did she know what to touch exactly? She did lightly, at times, like a feather, and forcefully at other times, as though she were angry at someone, yet she always made beautiful music.

When she left, I practised the tunes and chords by ear. I did the same at school, too, where Sister Teresa allowed me to play during recess and lunch.

« *Mais voyons donc!* » Mlle Hubert said one day, exasperated after Irene played her exercise. Even I knew that Irene had missed some notes. Mlle Hubert had demonstrated the exercise over and over again, each time beating the notes on the piano more and more forcefully until she sounded really angry.

When Father came in to pay Mlle Hubert, she whispered something, and they went to the kitchen. Following them, I caught the last part of her sentence. « *Sauvez votre argent pour d'autres choses* », she said. Save your money for something else.

"What are we to do with the piano," Mother asked Father as she served Mlle Hubert a cup of tea. "We still have a year of installments left to pay. Can we return it?"

"It's not like returning a shirt at Morgan's," Father said. "Remember how hard it was getting it upstairs."

Mlle Hubert might be able to find a buyer from her list of other students, she offered. I could already see them moving it down the circular metal staircase, and I wanted to cry.

"Don't sell it. I want to play it," I blurted out.

They laughed.

"You're still too young for lessons," Mother said, "and in three years, you might change your mind."

I sat at the piano and played effortlessly the last tune Irene had played so miserably.

« *Mais, voyons donc!* » Mlle Hubert said again, but this time with a smile.

Father picked me up, kissed me, and asked Mlle Hubert if she'd return next week to give me lessons.

It was one of those joyful moments that remains with you all through life, and it is that feeling of exhilaration I've strived for in my search for excellence—like dreaming of Gino performing at La Scala.

Though he came close to walking out on the maestro, Gino let his ego take a well-deserved break, for once.

"I did it for you," he told me later, "and sang directly at you as if you were sitting on the balcony across from the stage. Anyway, Marcello wouldn't give a horse's ass about the Maestro

Gino lives his roles to such an extent that, as Marcello, he overcame the petty arguments with the maestro. "Fight the dark with the light," I always tell him. Marcello did the rest.

If anything, the spats gave Gino more confidence to show off Marcello's devil-may-care attitude—the side of Gino that people love best. I taught him well! His performance was a tremendous success. Yet, I still wonder if the result would have been the same had sand a darker role, like Iago in Verdi's *Othello*. I do worry.

Gino plays a cocky Marcello. He also makes a sensational Escamillo, a boisterous Figaro, and a sparkling Don Giovanni. In Marcello, I've told him to roll these three qualities into one, but as a caring best friend to Rodolfo. It's the character that best suits his true nature.

Chapter 3
La petite Italienne
The 1940s

In my neighbourhood, they used to call me *la petite Italienne* because I only spoke Italian until I attended school. Once, I even heard a boy call me *la maudite Italienne*. At that time, many Quebecers still considered Italians uncultured peasants because many of the immigrants coming from Italy were unschooled and worked in menial jobs. But my father, Nicola Pizzolongo, who had emigrated in 1911 as a seventeen-year-old, taught us not to feel inferior or deny our origins. He might not have had high education, but he was born in Pescara in the Abruzzo region, close to Gioacchino Rossini's birthplace. Love of music, especially opera, was an inherited quality, part of his DNA. He may have been a simple marble cutter, but he revelled in his work in adorning beautiful residences, splendid public buildings, and the final resting places of people whose lives were honoured through the lasting beauty of marble. He had the heart of an artist. He could play the saxophone, trumpet, and violin, and he always sang around the house.

My maternal grandparents, Luigi and Carolina Ercolano, were also from Pescara and had emigrated in 1907. Their daughter Filomena married my father, and they settled in the Italian section of Montreal, near the Marché du Nord, now known as Marché Jean-Talon. Growing up, I remember listening to Toscanini on the radio on Saturday mornings, and the conductors Giuseppe and Guido Agostini lived in our neighbourhood. Giuseppe Agostini established a musical band, the Corpo Musicale Ordine Figli D'Italia, and started *Les futures étoiles* competition. I looked up to them and wished for a future filled with beautiful music and art.

Father often spoke of the artist Guido Nincheri, who created the most beautiful stained-glass windows in the province. He had designed the new Italian church, Madonna della Difesa, on Dante Street, where we went to mass every Sunday, which was renowned as one of the most beautiful churches built by the Italian clergy of America. The company where my father worked had provided the marble for the floor and walls of the church.

Later Nincheri worked at painting frescoes, and in 1933, when the fresco on the apse was inaugurated, the neighbourhood was abuzz about the figure of Mussolini on horseback along with Pope Pius XII. This was around the same time as the piano delivery, and I heard Mlle Hubert discussing Italian art with Father. She was the only person I knew who did not like the fresco on the ceiling of the church.

"There's no place for a politician in a church," she said, "just as there's no place for a crucifix in our National Assembly." She was not a fan of our Premier, Maurice Duplessis.

The frescoes had reawakened feelings of pride in the Italian community. That same year, in the *Crociera del Decennale,* Italo Balbo—Mussolini's right-hand man—led 24 seaplanes across the Atlantic, passing by Montreal en route to Lake Michigan and New York City. Celebrating his feat, Italians from the US and from Canada no longer felt ashamed to identify themselves as Italians.

Community members who delivered speeches on religious feasts had formed a committee a few years earlier to raise money for a cultural centre. The mayor, Camillien Houde, donated a parcel of land on Berri and Jean-Talon, not far from our home, and all the community's tradespeople—bricklayers, carpenters, electricians, plumbers and all—donated their time working on the construction of an Art Deco building named Casa D'Italia. Father volunteered his after-work hours laying a marble terrazzo floor with the insignia of the Fasci. At the time, we had no idea what the Fasci really meant; we only knew that it felt good being Italians in Montreal. Being called *la petite Italienne* felt more as a term of endearment than an insult.

All I cared about was studying piano and making my family, especially my father, proud of me. Mlle Hubert spurred me on, and I won prize after prize. I was a regular guest at the Ladies Morning Musical Club, and Mlle Hubert saw to it that the ladies contributed to my clothes, soliciting wealthy patrons like the Birks family, owners of Montreal's luxury jewellery store, so I was always well dressed for these occasions. When Professor Agostini heard me play, he told my father he considered me a child prodigy. At twelve, I won the French Government's Prix de Virtuosité and Montreal's prestigious Alfred Cortot Piano Scholarship to study in Paris with the best pianist and teacher in the world; World War II would interrupt those plans.

The piercing wails of police sirens shook the neighbourhood as I walked along Dante Street. Men were dragged from their homes and pushed into cars like criminals. These were the men who made speeches before processions at the Italian church, men who had hosted banquets and dances at the Casa D'Italia, friends of the mayor and other politicians. Why were they being arrested? Are they taking my father away, too?

I rushed home in fear, but there were no RCMP officers on our street. When father came home, he was terrified and furious. Mussolini had declared war on England. "He's gone mad," Father said, "and has taken us all down his crazy path." He blamed Mussolini and Italy, not the RCMP, but outside our house, he kept his opinions to himself. None of it made much sense to me.

We were thousands of miles from Italy, and most of the men arrested had been born and raised in Montreal. They had only joined the Fascist Party because it made them feel proud. Even the mayor of Montreal had exalted Mussolini.

How could everything change so suddenly? The community had just inaugurated the Casa D'Italia. The Italian church, Madonna della Difesa, was filled with frescoes and stained-glass windows. The community was finally achieving wealth and good things for its families, and we were also creating beautiful art. And now, overnight, we had turned into "enemy aliens."

All that the arrested men had in common was that they had supported the Fascist Party, some more strongly than others. They spared my family, as my father was apolitical. He had resisted joining a political party on the other side of the ocean and had not participated in political meetings at the Casa D'Italia; he had only attended the concerts held there by Giuseppe Agostini and his band.

People in our neighbourhood didn't talk out loud about the men's internment; it was as though there was some guilt attached to what had happened. Some of our Quebecois neighbours looked at us with suspicion, but my father told us, "Our conscience is clean. Our family has done nothing but contribute to the beauty of this country. Walk with your head high."

Repercussions from the war in Europe put a hold on my plans to study in Paris. Alfred Cortot, the most renowned classical musician of the twentieth century, had to flee Paris because of accusations over his role during the war. Though his wife was Jewish and he had helped many Jewish musicians during the German occupation in France, he had also played for the Germans, and was thus tainted with the allegation of having been a collaborator. He later defended himself in court, but Mlle Hubert was compelled to remove his name from her music school. "See what happens when politics mix with religion and now art?" she said to father. She was heartbroken, as was I over my lost opportunity.

I still dreamed of becoming a concert pianist, and my family did all they could to help me realize my dream. I graduated from the Montreal Conservatory, taught music, and played for Les Jeunesses Musicales du Québec Having won the Archambault Prize in 1943, I played many concerts sponsored by the Archambault music store. They displayed a poster with my picture on their store window on Sainte-Catherine and Berri Street for one of those concerts.

Chapter 4
Louis

As I listen to one of the most tender arias in opera, *"Che gelida manina,"* my heart fills with tenderness. Rodolfo and Mimi have just met in one of those unexpected moments that can change one's life and destiny. Marcello and his friends are off to the Café Momus to celebrate Christmas Eve, but Rodolfo stays behind to continue writing a poem. His words don't flow easily from his pen, however, and then his thoughts are interrupted by a timid knock on the door.

"Who's there?" he calls.

A woman's frail voice responds, *"Di grazia, mi si è spento il lume."* Her candle has gone out.

Rodolfo's candle also goes out, *"Oh Dio! Anche il mio s'è spento"*

Two spent candles, two penniless young people alone in a dark cold space illuminated only by the moonlight that steals through the window. Then a lost key. Rodolfo seizes that moment, finds the key, hides it in his pocket, and takes her cold hand in his. "Let me warm it into life," he sings.

Louis Quilico was a struggling young man longing to sing opera in spite of his family's opposition. When he saw my picture on a poster, he claims he fell instantly in love with me—or was it with the idea that he and I might be a pair? I often wondered that. But how Louis pursued me

16

and the idea! And when he heard the girl on the poster would be playing at a concert at the Windsor Hotel—he agreed to sing there.

Is it really possible to fall so quickly and hopelessly in love?

I did not.

It was 1949, and the war in Europe had ended. The invitation to play at the Windsor Hotel came from a group of Italian women who had established The Anita Garibaldi Society. Louis was accompanying the sister of a fellow singer, André Turp, at the event, but he hoped to strike up a friendship with me.

The Windsor Hotel was one of the most luxurious hotels in Montreal. Mlle Hubert saw to it I'd have the perfect evening dress for the event, a gift from the Birks family. When I made my entrance into the banquet hall, with its shimmering row of chandeliers, I felt like a princess at a ball. But really, I was a princess who had to perform for her meal, and I was a pack of nerves doing my best to look professional and collected. I had to show that the dress was not a waste of money for the Birks, nor the years of training a waste of money for Father and a waste of time for Mlle Hubert.

A good-looking but gawky fellow introduced himself as Louis and told me he had won the Saint Jean Baptiste opera contest. I was too pre-occupied to pay him much attention.

After he had sung his arias, Louis stayed close to me, a little too close. He had a strong voice, but it still needed some refinement, as did his clothes. His pants were baggy and his jacket was too big for his large frame, making him look even heftier than he was. He took up a lot of space with his easy, hearty laugh and got the most applause.

"We'd make a good duo," he said after he bowed to me yet again.

"I'm a concert pianist," I said. "I don't like playing duets with singers."

Rodolfo introduces himself to Mimi as a poet—"*Sono un poeta*"—who lives in penury, builds castles in the air, and dreams. "*Per sogni e per chimere, e per castelli in aria, l'anima ho milionaria,*" he declares. He is poor by choice but, in his soul, he feels like a millionaire.

After the concert at the Windsor Hotel, I saw Louis everywhere I went. He was so gregarious, and his laugh so contagious that I started opening up to him about music and performance. He had never studied music. His voice was a natural gift. He talked for hours about how badly he wanted to sing despite his father's objections. I was soon impatient with his sob stories.

"So, sing!" I told him. "If your father won't give you the money, go and work, find it another way. Don't just cry about it."

He needed that kick in the butt. At the urging of his choirmaster, I started giving Louis music lessons. His voice had potential, but he had made three unsuccessful attempts at a serious career before he met me and had given up.

"You've got a voice," I told him. "If you don't try, you'll regret it for the rest of your life."

I didn't know what to make of the awkward young baritone with the oversized jacket and the big voice. He was of Italian origin, like me, but I had never seen him at school, in church, or at any of the Italian feasts.

The Quilicos had little in common with my family. They were from Northern Italy and had little affinity with the rest of the community from Southern Italy. Also, Louis didn't speak Italian, for his mother, Jeanne Gravel, was French-speaking. At the time of our first meeting at the Windsor Hotel, the family lived in southeastern Montreal, close to the family business on Dorchester Street.

Louis spoke proudly of his grandfather, Antonio Quilico, who had travelled extensively as an engineer before emigrating to Canada to work on a railroad project. He spoke many languages and was known for his gregarious and entrepreneurial character. These qualities and his work on the railroads most likely gave my husband and son their love of model trains, their drive for movement, and their expansive attitude towards life.

In Italian families, the same names recur since firstborn sons are traditionally named after paternal grandfathers. The confusion created by this tradition was heightened in my husband's family because my father-in-law, Luigi, had named his son Louis, and we named our son Luigino, short for Luigi, and then further shortened the name to Gino. So, there are three Luigis in my story each named with a different variation on the name.

Luigi's love of motion led him to build a family business around bicycles—Bicycles Quilicot—which became a well-recognized establishment. When Luigi opened his bicycle store, he used the name Quilicot rather than Quilico because Montrealers so often viewed Italians as undesirable, and the *t* made the name look French. Louis had shown vocal talent and a love of music at an early age, but it was his father's interest in bicycles that powered the family. The business consumed him. "For him, there was only bicycles," Louis used to say. "No music." This father-son conflict lasted most of their lives. How I hoped Louis and Gino would never know such discord!

Louis's voice was a miracle of nature, and his success an even bigger miracle. When I met him, he was already consumed by a love of singing that had been sparked at school, when he was singled out to sing in a church choir. This is what led him to discover joy in singing—and the power of his voice. He sang all the time for himself and his friends, emulating the singers of the day, but it took a while before he took his singing seriously and started taking lessons.

I resisted tying myself romantically to Louis. I was too preoccupied with my own musical aspirations to commit to anyone, and I was still grieving the loss of a dashing airline pilot who had courted me for a short time before he left for duty in Europe. He had exuded elegance and promised a lifestyle that called for the kind of dress I wore at the Windsor Hotel, but he never returned from the war, and his body was never found. I thought I'd never want to fall in love with anyone else because it wouldn't be as special. And what if by some unforeseen chance my prince came back?

Would Louis and I ever have become a team if he had not seen the poster that led him to fall in love with me?

Our *gelida manina* moment happened one evening in the winter of 1949, during one of the biggest snowstorms of the year:

My parents had prepared a party to celebrate my birthday, but my heart was not in it. I was torn by feelings of uncertainty about what I really wanted out of life. More than anything else, I wanted a career as a concert pianist. I had worked too hard for years toward this goal to give it up. I had many friends but no real boyfriend yet. On the evening of my twenty-fourth birthday, I finally accepted that my pilot would never return from the war. I missed having a soulmate—someone to dance with, to talk to about music, to share my dream with. I wanted a world of music filled with imaginary loves, passions, jealousies. I longed for a fairy-tale love story, yet I was afraid to tie myself in a conventional marriage that would stand in the way of my dream.

These thoughts were running through my head as I helped my mother prepare to receive family for my birthday. Everyone ate, drank, danced, and laughed, except me. I played the piano not to entertain the guests but to distance myself from them and not have to talk and pretend to be happy. I'm terrible at faking my feelings, though, and my mother sensed my sadness. She tapped me on my shoulder and told me, "I forgot to invite your friend, the singer. Is it too late to do so?" I got to my feet, went to the kitchen with her, dialled his number, and gave her the phone. She invited Louis to come to the party. It was past 10:30, and a snowstorm was raging outside. He hesitated. Anyone would have been crazy to go out in such conditions, especially from the other side of downtown Montreal.

Frustrated by how I felt, I had little patience with his hesitation.

I pulled the phone from my mother's hand and yelled at him, "You're always pretending you love me so much. It's about time the man should prove his love for the woman."

And then I hung up.

I resigned myself to not seeing Louis that evening. "He's all talk," I decided, and I went back to playing furiously, holding back tears of frustration as everyone partied. At a quarter past twelve, the doorbell rang. I stopped playing, and everyone turned quiet. Louis appeared in the doorway, his clothes and hair wet from the snow, his cheeks red, and in his big generous voice said, « *Bon anniversaire, Lina.* »

I saw past the too large winter coat, dripping with snow, and saw the man I wanted to share my life with, the soul mate who shared the same love for music and the same desire to pursue the elusive and indefinable path to fame.

"*Mi chiamano Mimi,*" is how Mimi introduces herself to Rodolfo and tells him she loves all things that have gentle magic, that talk of love, of spring, that talk of dreams and fancies—the things called poetry—and then asks, "Do you understand me?"

He does. Their two minds meet and melt into one.

Still, I pursued a career and not marriage.

Chapter 5
On the Way
1949-1960

Alfred Cortot was back in Paris, and I finally had another chance to study with him in preparation for the Chopin international competition.

Louis was lost without me. He was so frustrated with his father and the business that he took the sudden and courageous decision to work on a boat feeding animals so he could go to Italy and study singing.

I like to think Louis broke away from his father to impress me. Not only did he take steps to cross the ocean and study music, but he had the courage to call me in Atlantic City where I'd gone with my parents for a short holiday before seeing me off to Europe from New York.

And then he arranged his travel plans to coincide with mine and asked me to meet him in New York!

We met in Central Park—two aspiring artists: I on my way to Paris; he on his way to Rome. We had no way of recognizing the prophetic symbolism of professing our love for each other in the city that would eventually launch Louis's career,

In late summer, a picnic in Central Park felt so thrilling for two poor souls like us. I packed salami and cheese sandwiches and two bottles of Coke. Louis couldn't stop talking about his trip to Italy. He wasn't yet sure what he'd find once there—but where else would he find the best teachers of opera singing? He was euphoric, certain his gamble would pay off. His eyes sparkled with pride as he opened a small gift box and offered it to me as a sign of his love.

"Will you marry me?" he asked.

He had spent the largest amount of money he could afford, $14.78, on a gold ring. I had never wanted to play for a singer, let alone marry one—and an impoverished one at that—but the expression of love was so sincere and his determination to risk all in his search to perfect his art so strong that I fell under the spell of those kind, hopeful eyes, those large arms and shoulders that would protect and hug my dreams as well.

I said yes and tied myself forever to a baritone.

"*Oh soave fanciulla/* Thou beauteous maiden!" Rodolfo takes Mimi in his arms and they sing a passionate duet that will echo throughout the opera, like the leitmotif of true love built not only on physical passion but on the mutual pursuit of beauty and art.

"Ah! Love, you rule alone!" Mimi tells Rodolfo. "I'll stay close to you."

Louis knew no one in Rome, spoke no Italian, and slept on a mattress on the floor at a convent, he told me during our weekly phone calls. He had gone to study singing, and he did so with Riccardo Stracciari, a famous baritone. Meanwhile, I was studying in Paris with Cortot, who surprised me by being concerned less with technique than with interpretation and the emotion stirred by the music. It was exciting and exhilarating, yet I looked at that $14.78 ring, and I heard Louis's voice call out for me.

Paris was cold and damp, and I came down with a bad case of bronchitis.

"It's beautiful and sunny here," Louis told me.

My own road led me to Rome.

We argued as we got ready on the morning of our wedding.

"Where are you going?" Louis asked me as I was getting dressed.

"The same place as you."

We hopped in a taxi and were married at Saint Peter's.

It happened without our families, and at seven-thirty in the morning—which was the only time the cardinal would marry us. Was it because he feared we had lived in sin and I would not be wearing a white dress and veil that he did not want us to marry in the brighter light of day? We didn't bother asking.

We lived as dirt-poor students but felt lucky to have each other. We found a landlady, Signora Valeri, who took a liking to us. She was a quiet woman dressed in black who loved music and opera but who had had little joy since her son had never returned from the war. Louis reminded her of him, she later told us, and she treated us not as boarders but as the son and daughter-in-law she had lost. She made sure I didn't do any chores around the place for fear of hurting my precious fingers, and she shared her meals with us.

Our time in Rome was fundamental for the development of Louis's voice. But money was more and more difficult to come by. We relied on the help of my grandparents, the Ercolan os. My parents didn't have the money, the province of Quebec didn't come through with the scholarship we had hoped for, and Louis's father refused our request for support.

When our money ran out, we had no choice but to return to Montreal, but life was not much easier there. Louis's relationship with his father got worse when his father separated from his mother and lived with another woman. The children took sides, and so the family was splintered. Moreover, the City of Montreal had expropriated their building on Dorchester Street and the family together with Bicycles Quilicot moved north to Saint Michel, before the business moved to its more permanent location on Saint Denis.

I pushed him to rise beyond the petty family squabbles through music. I found another coach, Martial Singher, a leading baritone at the Met. I believed in Louis; my family believed in him and helped us as much as they could. He entered and won the CBC Futures étoiles competition and a contract to sing on the radio and concerts in cities around Quebec.

All this paid off when he was offered a scholarship to study at the Mannes College of Music, and we returned to New York. Pregnant with our first child, I took on a job playing piano for a 40-perfomance tour of *The Barber of Seville*.

Our daughter Donna Maria was born in 1951—a joy for both of us, but how we struggled financially! Louis worked as an elevator operator at the Statler Hotel, from eleven o'clock at night to eight o'clock in the morning so he could study during the day. He'd be ready for lessons from Professor Singher from ten to four, then sleep, and repeat.

All this for $43 a week.

I made big soups for dinners, which I diluted so they'd last all week. Still, we couldn't make ends meet until my parents sold their home in Montreal and bought a large house in Flushing Meadows, New York, and moved there to be with us. Our new home came with a fireplace, an eighteen by forty-five-foot living room big enough for a grand piano—the concert hall of our dreams!

An opera singer's career, like his voice, takes years to develop. Had it not been for these sacrifices we all made as a family, my insistence, and Louis's perseverance, he would have fallen by the wayside like many other talented artists. It was during those first difficult years in Flushing, New York, that Louis's career took shape.

One day, he was anxious and nervous when he got home; I could tell by the way he moved and stuttered. His teacher had arranged for him to audition for the Metropolitan Opera on Air. "It's a momentous opportunity," I told him. "You should be excited."

"I'm not ready. What if I fail? I'll never get a second chance again. I'm scared."

"Your chance has come now. Get yourself ready! We made a deal when we married to make music our living."

And he won, against all odds!

The win garnered publicity in Canada and an article in *The New Yorker*. After a contract with the New York City Opera, he was offered a contract to sing a San Francisco opera season.

The season included five different operas. He knew *La Bohème*, but had neither sung nor even seen any of the other four. Again, he panicked, haunted by doubts over his ability to undertake such a contract, but this time he tackled his demons alone. Louis had come to appreciate that his body was his only instrument, but the body has so many mysterious parts and openings, vulnerable to weather, health, even mood. He always worried that his instrument would betray him.

"What is singing all about?' he asked me one day.

"After all the lessons from Professor Singher, and so many others, you still don't know?"

"I have followed instructions without really understanding what I'm doing. I want to know how the body produces the sounds, how to master my breath to make the singing seem effortless, how to tell these hidden organs what to do, so my body won't ever let me down."

To be totally in control, I told him, to own the voice without fear or doubt, he needed first to understand its genesis in his mind before the voice moves from his guts to the vocal cords to its final expression.

How he found the power of his voice and the assurance that he could conquer the world of opera was almost otherworldly.

One morning, I heard him practising in his studio, as usual, but he had closed the door, which he never did. When I opened the door to call him for lunch, he didn't respond. He seemed lost in his own world, singing with his eyes closed a few feet from the wall. I left him there but checked on him from time to time. He never even heard me, so intense was his concentration.

When it was close to supper time, I called out, "Louis, you've been practising for eight hours."

He looked disoriented and I ran towards him just in time to catch him as he fell down in my arms.

"I want to understand," he said.

Years later, Louis would say that the four most important and happy events in his life were the birth of his two children, winning the Met audition, and the self-discovery of the power of his voice beside that wall in our house in Flushing Meadows, New York. It was this self-determination that more than any other quality helped him overcome many stumbling blocks. The San Francisco debut brought him the attention of the critics as a Verdian baritone to watch.

It was not only Louis's career that benefitted from those difficult early years. Gino's career and, in a way, my own benefitted, as well. Would Gino ever have studied opera if his father had not made it as an opera singer? Could I have made it as a solo concert pianist on my own? Yes, I sacrificed the chance to find out, but I fully embraced Louis's career and, in so doing, became part of it, just as I feel part of Gino's as I sit in my imaginary second-row balcony at La Scala and reliving my own life through Mimi's.

It's the end of the first act, and Rodolfo asks, "Tell me you love me!"

"I love you," Mimi replies.

Rodolfo and Mimi sing together as they walk out, "*Amor, amor, amor.*"

Chapter 6
The Children

Puccini's music elicits many of the memories and places that Louis's career took us—the children packed and dragged along like suitcases. They developed their own distinct personalities and stories, though the more immediate needs of our ambitious pursuits may sometimes have taken centre stage. Listening to Gino's voice of his recording of *La Bohème*, I reflect on his growth from a gentle, shy child to a gregarious and fun-loving Marcello.

It's in Scene Two that he shows his natural swagger as the lively group of friends meets outside Café Momus in the Latin Quarter of Paris. This is one of the most exuberant scenes in opera, with vendors, students, children, and jugglers packing the square celebrating Christmas. Marcello revels at the attention of the girls crowding around him, offering his love to all the cheerful ladies—not at all a difficult role for Gino.

"*Chi vuol, donnine allegre, un po' d'amor?* / Which of you cheerful ladies desires some love?" he sings. He is in love with Musetta, a beautiful courtesan who lives off a wealthy old man. Marcello tries to hide his jealousy when she makes a flamboyant entrance in rich clothes, followed by the aged Alchidoro. Later, he tells Mimi that laughter and song are the secret of a lasting love. "*Ci amiamo in allegria* / We love light-heartedly." Gino displays his most cynical smirk in this scene. He has had his share of Musettas.

There are times when Gino's cheekiness is perceived as arrogance, but I know better. He was not always so overconfident. Though mischievous, he was sensitive, soft-spoken, and gentle. Unlike Louis's robust male physicality, Gino grew slender and delicate, more like me.

Donna, three years his senior, was a feisty and strong-willed child. She showed an early love of dancing and drawing, and I enrolled her in dancing lessons as soon as she was of age. Like all siblings, Donna and Gino fought over their toys. Gino would steal and undress her Barbie dolls to get her mad, and she retaliated by playing tricks on him, like adding salt in his milk. But they were inseparable, especially after we started moving around the world and they had only each other as playmates.

When he turned three and Donna six, in 1958, we were obliged to return to Montreal. The recognition Louis had had in the U.S. did not translate easily into enough money to feed a family of four. His father was as reluctant as ever to help us out, refusing to acknowledge the successes Louis had had in his young career and insisting that he return to Montreal, where he had a secure job at the bicycle store.

We had no choice but to pack our bags and work for our meals at whatever menial occupation was available. Changing and pumping bicycle tires, greasing sprockets and chains were all that Luigi had to offer his son.

Gino loved visiting the store. In the alley, he could climb his grandfather's truck and pretend to drive it. And one day he took the pretending a little too far.

Gino was enthralled by the garbage trucks in the back alley—the *ruelle*—and the garbage men who jumped up and down off the ledge of their trucks and yelled "*vidanges.*" He was mesmerized by how the garbage bags disappeared into the truck and were eaten up by giant rotating blades. His grandfather's truck parked in the alley, Gino climbed in and decided to be a garbage man himself. He yelled "*vidanges*" and turned the key his grandfather had left in the ignition. The noise scared the wits out of him and all of us. He quickly got out of the truck, while his grandfather jumped in to turn off the ignition.

I was less enamoured with the pattern of our life in Montreal. I had to remain a silent bystander to my father-in-law's mean-spiritedness towards Louis. Luigi demonstrated his displeasure with Louis in many small ways. He owned a Lincoln Continental, proof of his financial success. While Louis's brother, Toni, was allowed to drive it, Louis could not get close to it.

Luigi's oppressive behaviour was felt by other members of the family as well, especially the girls. Madeleine, Louis's youngest sister, decided to enter a convent just to get away from the family's squabbles and conflicts. He was hard on all the children, and there was constant arguing.

The tension between father and son kept worsening the more Luigi discouraged Louis from pursuing a singing career. "He can't accept that you will surpass him and break out from his hold on the family," I told Louis.

I feared that the longer we remained there, the harder it would be for Louis to break free and follow his dream, especially given the sacrifices we had made in Rome and New York. And what had happened to my own career goals, to the sparkle of the chandeliers in the Windsor Hotel, that place where we first met and that had held the promise of music, recitals, and applause for both of us?

It became clear that Louis could not survive in Montreal and pursue a career as an opera singer on his bicycle shop salary. Out of desperation, he opened his own bicycle store to compete with his father—a decision that meant they stopped speaking to each other for ten years. In retrospect, I can see how that conflict defined Louis in many ways: his brash and buoyant physical posture disguised vulnerabilities that reflected his poor relationship with his father.

For the children the bicycle store was a playroom full of tricycles, pedal cars, and the miniature train sets their father had collected for years. However, I didn't hide my unhappiness at seeing Louis get his hands greasy. I had never regretted giving up my career to build his, and in some ways I still lived the artist's life through my husband, but I started resenting my choice as Louis got more and more involved in his bicycle store.

"Do or die," I told him. "I did not give up my career to work next to a grease monkey."

To my relief, Louis's bicycle store went bankrupt, which forced him to close, though the debt would weigh on us for years. To my greater relief, his reputation was beginning to rise, together with those of other Canadian singers like Richard Verreau, André Turp, Robert Savoie, and Joseph Rouleau. And then, in 1961, Covent Garden offered him a contract.

We packed our bags for London together with my now-widowed mother, whom the children called Nanni. She would live with us and help take care of the household and children.

The move to London was a significant advance in Louis's career, certainly. I do ask myself how the frequent dislocations affected Gino and Donna? Was I too involved in Louis's career even to consider the effect our many moves had on them?

In Montreal, the children heard and spoke mostly French and Italian. Now, they had to learn English. Not quite six, Gino was not yet at school, so he spent hours on his own, living a fantasy life with his budgie, his trains, and his thoughts. Donna started ballet classes, which she loved. But neither child had a chance to develop deep friendships in London. Though they were accustomed to their father singing in the house, Louis's musical career can't have meant much to them at that time. They simply took for granted the fact that their father sang *La Traviata* next to Joan Sutherland, that he received flowers after his performance of *Rigoletto* (something normally only reserved for female singers), that we were finally without financial worries—and even able to take holidays in Switzerland and Italy. At the time, I never wondered how discombobulating it must have been for a child as young as Gino to be torn away from his own huge toy store.

We took many decisions to further Louis's career, some of which, in retrospect, might not have been the best for the children. Just as they were coming to terms with English, Louis got a house contract to sing at the Paris Opera, and in 1962, we all moved to Paris. So Gino started school in Paris when he was seven, and he often came home crying because his schoolmates made fun of him for being different. He was even ridiculed and once slapped by his teacher, who belittled him for looking American in his baseball cap. I told him I had also been mocked in Montreal for looking Italian, but I hadn't let it bother me.

"The harassment will stop if you believe in yourself and don't let the opinion of others affect how you feel," I told him. That's the philosophy I have lived by, and it has served me well.

To help the children understand why we had moved to Paris, I took them to see their father perform at the Paris Opera. It was the first time they had ever seen him on stage.

The children were dressed up in new clothes—a crinoline dress and black patent leather shoes for Donna, and a black suit, white shirt, and bow tie for Gino. I was worried that they might get bored and made plans to leave early, if necessary.

Place de l'Opéra was all lit up for the premiere of *Don Carlos*. I watched the children's behaviour for possible signs of restlessness. Donna followed quietly; Gino seemed to be lost as he stared in amazement at the highly ornamented façade of the Palais Garnier, which was considered a *"monument historique,"* with its multicoloured marble friezes, columns, and statuary. For once, I entered the theatre by the front entrance rather than backstage. I took the children on a tour of the place that inspired the novel The *Phantom of the Opera* and the silent horror movie with Lon Cheney of that same name. I walked them up the grand staircase and the Grand Foyer, explaining that the large paintings represented various moments in the history of music. The auditorium was richly decorated in velvet and gold leaf, with sumptuous paintings of cherubim and nymphs. I pointed to the seven-ton chandelier in bronze and crystal, shimmering with its thousand lights, the largest I had ever seen. Gino's face lit up in awe.

"Wow!" he kept repeating at everything he saw. "Does a king live here?"

"Your father lives here... for a while... when he sings." I didn't want to dispel the magic of the place and the moment. Minutes later, Gino jumped up from his seat, standing up in admiration and clapping excitedly when he saw his father appear on stage in full costume as the Marquis de Posa. I smiled.

Of that performance, the music reviewer of *France-Soir* wrote:

De toute la distribution, seul le baryton Canadien, Louis Quilico, est tout à fait digne de son rôle celin du Marquis de Posa.

In other words, Louis's performance was remarkable.

Chapter 7
Rome

After Louis established a firm reputation in Paris, we moved on to Rome in 1965. Gino was not ten years old, and he and Donna had already lived the life of bohemians in five countries—Canada, US, England, France, and Italy—where Gino would later work several times when he himself became as an opera singer.

We led a near-normal family life in Rome, perhaps for the first time. We rented a modern apartment in the EUR district, a new section of Rome built by Mussolini before the war to host an International World Fair. The imposing Conference Centre and many public buildings and squares built in the architectural style of the Fascist regime, which was itself inspired by ancient Roman architecture, were meant to show off the Fascist empire to the world. Neither the Fair nor the glory of victory was ever realized, but the wide Cristoforo Colombo Avenue, built at the same time, still made it possible to drive directly from l'EUR to the beach in Ostia in less than forty-five minutes. We rented a house on the beach with a boat which we used in our free time. Gino loved the new lifestyle—the sun, the drives to the beach in our convertible car, all of us singing.

Rome was abuzz with American tourists experiencing their own *dolce vita*, and there were many American military families nearby, as well. To avoid further language confusion, we chose private American schools—Notre Dame for Gino and Marymount for Donna. We had the best of many worlds in Rome and were fascinated by its ancient, medieval, and baroque history, the exuberance of the jetsetters on Via Veneto, and the familiar pleasures of living in a modern apartment with American families.

Gino took well to the school, which was a one-hour drive away, and he started making friends. Up to this point, he had listened to classical music at home, but he now discovered pop and rock music and made friends with a boy who played guitar. It was the heyday of the Beatles and the Rolling Stones, and we allowed Gino to attend his first rock concert at l'EUR to see the Rolling Stones.

Both children enjoyed a lot of freedom in Rome and were able to go anywhere without fear of street violence. We brought them with us for late-night dinners at restaurants, and they often ended up sleeping in the car. Gino's popularity was much enhanced by the fact he was the only boy in his circle who owned a motorized scooter—a Solex. He still listened to Mario Lanza together with the Beatles and the Rolling Stones. It was a glorious and innocent time for all of us, and especially for Gino, who had his first crush on a girl who lived in our complex.

And then, on the very cusp of adolescence, Gino's carefree life in Rome was ripped away from him when we made the sudden and drastic decision to move back to New York.

The reason for this move was a family situation none of us could have predicted—nothing to do with Louis's career, for once. It's a situation we kept very much to ourselves.

Gino and Donna had both spent the summer of 1966 at a camp in Sardinia. As we crossed the water on a ferry to pick them up and I enjoyed the warm sun on my face, I felt blessed that we had finally found the right balance between professional success for Louis and peace and harmony for the family. When we arrived at the camp, Gino was his cheerful and mischievous self, while Donna seemed to be in a lousy mood and bawled at everything we said.

"You should be grateful, young lady," I scolded her. "You've spent a wonderful summer in such a beautiful place."

"I think I'm pregnant!"

There was a long, painful pause when no one seemed to know what to say. She was barely fifteen and Gino was eleven; they were two children at the end of summer camp. "You're only a child," I said finally. "It can't be."

Donna burst into tears, and I was afraid she was not making this up. We had been living in a romanticized world of opera and make-believe.

The hard fact that I had been oblivious to the reality of Donna's development from child to woman hit me in the face. I felt sudden guilt rather than anger at my daughter.

Once the shock of the news subsided, my concern was how to help Donna, a child herself, deal with the situation with the least possible negative effect on her life. The father, Paul, was a sixteen-year-old Italian-American living in Rome. Out of religious and moral beliefs, abortion was not an option and, even if it had been, I certainly would never have considered having my fifteen-year-old daughter go to some clandestine back-alley butcher and risk her emotional and physical health.

We came together as a family and devised a strategy. Donna and Paul were married, but we didn't want Donna to stop her education. The mores at the time in Italy were such that we felt Donna might be scarred socially. How would she be judged in conservative Italy and within her group of friends in school? I was now questioning whether the life we had led so far had been worth the havoc it wreaked on the children. Had the innocent, carefree life in Rome been only a delusional interlude before reality set in?

My mother's ultimate dream had been to own a home with an indoor staircase. In my newly troubled state of mind, I was keenly aware of the lack of a solid, physical house where we could feel safe and secure. When under stress, we often make decisions that might not be the most rational. I didn't want Donna to raise a baby in Italy while going to school and living in an apartment. After a discussion with Louis, we decided to return to North America and build a more permanent base.

The effect of this move on Gino and Donna lasted for years. At the time, though, we followed our instincts and did what we considered best for all. Louis would continue travelling, but the children and baby would have a house they could call home. We bought a sprawling house in Long Island, New York. It was a turning point for us all.

New York City in 1967 was not the Flushing Meadows we had left in 1958. It was abuzz with rock and roll, antiwar demonstrations, and the Summer of Love. Our emotional baggage was both heavier and more fragile. Donna carried a baby while Gino was going through puberty, not an easy time under the best conditions. These would be his most rebellious years.

A few months after arriving in New York, Donna gave birth to a little boy, and we welcomed him with joy. Donna chose the name David. From a book on names and their significance, I learned that David was "the loved one." His father, Paul, had decided to stay behind in Rome and continue his education there, and for personal reasons, he later renounced the child, and we were able, because of this, to get the marriage annulled. Even in New York, we didn't want Donna to sacrifice a chance at a normal life, so we encouraged her to continue her studies and ballet classes, and we took care of David as if he were our own child. This was an unusual arrangement, but no one questioned it in New York, where we had developed some professional relationships but had few close friends.

Chapter 8
Recognition at Home

Louis's career flourished in North America and provided the sense of permanence I had wanted for our family. He still maintained a presence in the European opera houses for the first year or so after the move, then slowly scaled that back.

By this time, he was singled out time and again as the Canadian Verdian baritone *par excellence,* especially for the heavier Verdi operas like *Aida, Falstaff, Il Trovatore, Macbeth, Otello, Rigoletto.* He appeared regularly with the Canadian Opera Company and the CBC, and in time was offered a teaching position at the Faculty of Music of the University of Toronto. He agreed to teach one singing class per month as long as he could arrange his performance schedule around it. I later took over the course when he was not available. This was an ideal arrangement for me, as I always loved teaching, and I could see myself doing it for many more years.

With this in mind, in 1969, we moved to Toronto and made that our home base while Louis travelled to New York. Four years later, in 1973, he signed a permanent contract with the Metropolitan Opera. He achieved the height of his career at the Met, performing next to the world's most celebrated conductors and singers while we worked as a team complementing each other in our teaching. At times, we disagreed on technique, but we both loved working with young people.

Eventually, we each taught our separate classes. Over the years, we pulled together and developed our own "Nine Rules of the Quilico Studio" which brought together basic operatic techniques that had taken Louis and me a lifetime to perfect, focusing on: posture, the abdomen muscles, breathing, opening and expansion of the throat, resonance, the eyes, awareness and cosciousnes, and finally, making the sound.

As Louis's career and mine stabilized into a comfortable and more serene pace, our children grew up in the shadow of their father's successes, struggling to find their own place in the world. It would be a few more troubled years in New York and Toronto before Gino experienced his musical awakening and finally found his way into the superb musical career he craved for himself. As a handsome and restless young man, he had his share of disappointments, passionate love stories, betrayals, jealousies, and doubts. A failed first marriage at a very young age threw him a curve early on but did not thwart his progress. When his career took off, he met and married beautiful Kathryn Stephenson and blessed us with two more grandchildren.

Donna studied ballet seriously with Les Grand Ballets canadiens de Montréal while we looked after baby David, but she then gave that up in order to be closer to her son. She suffered through several emotional years and a series of failed relationships, and did eventually remarry, but her second husband, Franco, did not have a steady income. When their daughter Natasha was born, I had an extension built to our house, and we all lived under the same roof. Gino and his first girlfriend lived with us before they married, too. At times, the place seemed more like the Grand Hall of Toronto's Union Station with Louis and Gino coming and going, baby David growing up before our eyes, then, as a teen, entertaining his friends.

When we were all at home, the noise was often above the decibel level of any opera chorus, especially when Louis and Gino rehearsed their roles in booming voices meant to project in large theatres for thousands of spectators. Conflicts between siblings living in such close proximity were at times inevitable. Donna and Franco often butted heads with Gino. To break the tension, I'd run to the piano, and just as inevitably, Louis and Gino would break into song. It's how we settled our differences, with music and song. Aside from occasional outbursts, we supported each other well.

Donna and Franco eventually expressed their desire to be on their own, which we encouraged, but we were saddened to hear of their decision to move to Italy, where Franco still had family. We were worried about uprooting David, and he, a teen by this time, chose to remain with us in Toronto. He had also considered singing for a while, then turned to composing and pursued studies in music at York University

For Louis and me, life could not have been better. To give something back, I got involved in a fundraising project that started with a simple request by Father Cellini, a Toronto representative of the Consolata Missions, to help organize a concert to raise money for Kenya's mission work. It developed into the *Water for Africa* series of concerts that raised funds to supply wells, generators, pipes, aqueducts, reservoirs, and dams to provide water for schools and hospitals in Kenya, Mozambique, Ethiopia. Some of the concerts, held in old Massey Hall, were televised by the CBC and provided a platform for talented young singers from Canada and across the world. We even organized some concerts in Italy with plans to expand in other countries. Louis and I had the privilege to visit the African missions to see for ourselves how the money helped people who lived without the basic necessities of life. It became a project very dear to my heart.

Meanwhile, Louis continued receiving accolades and excellent reviews—far too many to mention here. Gino's career was also blossoming. In 1988, Louis and Gino made history at the Met in an extraordinary father/son performance. But the one concert that stands out for me above any other was held, not in a grand opera house, but in a sports arena in Montreal where Louis, Gino, and I performed as a family.

The mayor of Montreal, Jean Drapeau, had invited us to perform at the opening of the Montreal's Symphony Pop Concerts conducted by Charles Dutoit. It was a thrill as this first special concert had been advertised to honour the Quilico family. Despite his busy schedule, Gino flew from Toulouse to be with us. We knew that many of our friends and relatives in Montreal would be there but didn't know what else to expect of the evening.

We drove towards the Maurice Richard Arena in Montreal's east end in a Jaguar belonging to Gino's good friend, Victor Melnikoff, but the traffic was so heavy we grew anxious. As we neared the arena, we were blocked by a bottleneck of heavy traffic, and Louis lost his cool.

"Who would have thought there'd be traffic in this part of town, and why tonight of all nights?" Jean Drapeau was one of his most loyal fans, and Louis didn't want to disrespect him and Charles Dutoit by showing up late.

"It's because of the Expos' baseball game at the Olympic Stadium," Gino said. "I'm afraid we'll be singing to an empty arena tonight, Dad."

This comment having exacerbated Louis's nervousness, Gino added, "Don't worry, your friend Drapeau will understand. He'll be more than happy to see his baby filled up."

Then he and Victor joked about the Mayor and the embarrassing crisis that followed the construction of the stadium for the 1976 Montreal Olympics. The Mayor's prediction that, "The Olympics can no more lose money than a man can have a baby," became a running joke with the citizens of Montreal that had to bear the heavy debt for the stadium's cost overruns .

"All dreams cost money," Louis said. "Drapeau has vision and imagination and does not put a dollar sign on culture."

As we reached the parking entrance of the arena, still moving at a snail's pace, someone came out of a car and yelled, "It's the Quilicos!"

People started running towards our car as if we were rock stars. It dawned on us that the rush of people had all been driving to the Arena for our concert!

Once we arrived, we had time to calm our nerves. The concert started late because the crowd was still lined up to purchase tickets.

"Here come the father, the son, and the holy spirit," Gino joked as we got ready to enter the stage. We were greeted enthusiastically by a standing ovation from the arena packed with more than 6,500 fans. More than 1,500 other fans had to be turned away.

They gave me the same space at the concert as Louis and Gino. It was the first time in 25 years that I had played as a soloist. I saw myself again as a little girl playing the piano for Mlle Hubert and my parents. I felt no regrets for how my life had turned out, only gratitude. I played my heart out that evening to an audience that was of utmost important to me, my family, my friends, and the Montreal fans who had believed in all of us.

The Mayor planned a reception after the concert with the Ambassador of France and many distinguished local dignitaries, and we were very late for that special occasion. I had not wanted to rush all the friends and family that came backstage to hug us. I hadn't seen some of them for more than 25 years.

My dreams had all come true, and I felt fulfilled. We had had many ups and downs, some of them painful to remember. If only the moments of pure bliss could be bottled and made to last to make up for the years of struggle.

I'll end my story here, with my eyes closed. I'll savour every note sang and played to perfection while following the rest of the artists' story, as if for the very first time. Listening to *La Bohème* has made me relive our own years of hunger and drive. In retrospect, they were the most beautiful because they were so full of expectation and hope.

The gods were not so kind to Rodolfo and Mimi. She becomes very ill, and Rodolfo cannot offer her the care she needs. They separate not for lack of love but for lack of the basic sustenance of life—a problem that has crushed the dreams of many young artists. Both Musetta and Mimi are compelled to spend their time with wealthier suitors, far from the loves of their lives.

In the last act, winter has ended, and we find Marcello and Rodolfo where it all started, alone in the garret. Rodolfo pines for Mimi: "*Ah! Mimì, mia breve gioventù.*" Ah! Mimì! My short-lived youth.

Marcello dreams of Musetta: "*Se pingere mi piace/o cieli o terre/o inverni o/primavere,/egli mi traccia due pupille nere/e una bocca procace,/e n'esce di Musetta il viso ancor.../* Whether I want to paint earth or sky, spring or winter, the brush outlines two dark eyes and inviting lips, and Musetta's face appears..."

Then Musetta and Mimi do appear. Mimi is dying of consumption, but happy to be back in the garret where she had found happiness. She has no delusions about her condition: "*Bella come un'aurora,*" Rodolfo sings on seeing her—beautiful like a dawn.

Mimi replies, "*Volevi dir: bella come un tramonto/* You meant beautiful like a sunset."

"*Mi chiamano Mimì,*" she sings, breathing her last sigh of happiness.

Chapter 9
Vissi D'Arte; Vissi D'Amore

Mimi died too young. With any premature death, we suffer not only the pain of loss but also at the thought of our own unrealized dreams. The death of a young person raises many "what ifs."

What if Rodolfo had become a famous author and Mimi remained a poor seamstress? Would their love have survived?

What if—in spite of their continued poverty and lack of success—Mimi and Rodolfo had married, had had children, grandchildren. What kind of life would that have been? Would they have been happy with each other?

What if Mimi had died at age 66, after she and Rodolfo had achieved their artistic dreams, extending those dreams to their children and grandchildren. What would she want to remember, forget, tell?

And what if the life you have lived and all that you have striven for is suddenly pulled away from you?

I was diagnosed with liver cancer as I was helping Gino prepare for his La Scala debut. There is nothing like a cancer diagnosis to make one reflect on the life you have lived. It was the story of our life that played out on the *La Bohème* stage, and my son sang it. Strange, though, that the scenes that came across most clearly were not of the huge successes achieved by both Louis and Gino, but of the icy staircase, the fourteen dollar ring, the bicycle store, our first home in Flushing Meadows, our concert as a family at a hockey arena in Montreal.

I held out as well as I could after Gino's return from Milan, because I didn't want to put a damper on his and Louis's scheduled performances. During my illness, I learned not to interfere with the natural flow of life and let things be. We all knew that my illness would be getting the better of me before very long.

My condition had the effect of turning the tables on me. I had always taken care of everyone, and now the family had to take care of me. I didn't like it one bit, having to depend on others. But I hid my discomfort. What would make me happiest, I insisted, was that they respect their artistic commitments.

Louis become sad and haggard—he who loved to laugh. My illness took its toll on him, and he was utterly unprepared for the role reversal, though I did all I could to keep my spirits up so the others would not fall to pieces.

I chose to enter an experimental protocol and be treated at home. Donna returned from Italy to be with me. Together with David and Gino's wife, Kathryn, she nursed me while Louis and Gino maintained their singing engagements. David and Donna took me to my doctor's appointments and treatments, while Kathryn was the one who connected me intravenously for my medication.

By September, the signs of my illness were intensifying, and I was drugged with narcotics. I heard Gino argue with his father about cancelling his next scheduled performance of *Don Giovanni* at the San Francisco Opera Company. He wanted to cancel, whereas Louis told him he should pack up and go, that he could make a hasty return to Toronto if need be. I nodded in agreement.

"I want to stay with you until you get better," he told me.

I disapproved. The show had to go on while I was still breathing. It was a Quilico unwritten rule of law that one cannot cancel a concert!

"Your mother wants you to sing, not sit here and weep before it's time," Louis told him. "Go and sing for her."

As soon as he left, I fell into a deep coma.

I could hear Louis talk to me, beg me to speak to him, but I could not respond, I felt my family's presence, but I could not see them. From the shuffling of feet, the sobbing, light kisses and touches, I knew my time had come.

Gino's instincts not to leave me had been correct. He called as soon as he arrived in San Francisco. Kathy was beside me and put the phone receiver on my ear. As I heard Gino's voice, I took my last feeble breath. I felt a sense of perfect peace as I saw myself move through a dark tunnel toward a bright, glorious light.

And that's how I joined those who have loved and been loved so much that their spirit lingers over the people that have given them reasons for living.

Grieving mortals don't realize that we never quite leave our loved ones. Our sad fate is that our earthy embodiments remain frozen in time, like statues of salt, stalagmites, without the faculty of movement or action. All we can do is watch and remain forever what we once were.

Do our loved ones feel our presence? Many never look for us, so indeed, they never do. Others, who have the talent to live in a dream, to perceive life in third dimensions, will experience the presence of our spirits over, behind, beside them, and never let us die.

Does one ever die after having invested so much in living? Like Mimi, who is a creation of all that is beauty, the poetry remains; it cannot die! As mortals, we become immortal through our contribution to life and especially to art.

Gino cancelled his first performance and rushed home only to find me gone. Everyone in the Canadian opera world was at the beautiful funeral that Father Cellini presided over. A children's choir sang like angels and made me feel completely at home in my new dimension.

Father and son and the rest of the family were grief-stricken. It saddened me to feel their sense of loss and emptiness. For once, though, I couldn't tell them to pull themselves together; after our spirit separates from our bodies, our destiny is complete silence and invisibility.

When I was a child, our religious teachers taught us that the afterlife would be spent in either paradise, purgatory, or hell. It can be all of those things, as we, who are our own harshest judges, weigh in on whether our contribution on earth has been worthy.

Our lives' final reckoning is also measured by the happiness or havoc we have caused those who have been part of our lives or whose paths we have crossed. It's heaven when we look down and see loved ones live happy lives while keeping loving memories of our time together. Call us angels, if you like, as our spirits float about and rejoice with all others whose lives have had such merit. It's purgatory when we see our people struggle to search for their reasons for living, when we can no longer help point them in the right direction. Complete numbness and quiet reigns as we wait for some sign that we have not failed them and thus failed ourselves. It's hell, complete with screeches of anguish and pain, when we see people lose sight of what you have meant for them, or—worse still—when they blame their sufferings on the part you have played on their lives, convincing you that your own life on earth was futile.

Being above the daily grind of living that so often obfuscates our perceptions, I like to sum up my life in a few words, as best expressed by the great Puccini: "*Vissi d'arte; vissi d'amore....*" I lived in search of art, beauty, and excellence in music, and I found all that. I also lived for love—love for Louis and my family. I left Louis and Gino at the top of their form, brought father and son to the Met and Gino to La Scala where Mimi dies of consumption. And I with her.

Chapter 10
Coraggio

Who does not feel a pang at the last scene of *La Bohème*? It destroys me, Gino, every time I'm in it. I cry real tears at the ending of this opera. At my debut at La Scala, the tears came accompanied by pain at the prospect of my great loss and with thoughts of my own mortality.

I left for Milan with the spectre of death and calamity over me, brooding over unanswerable questions about the meaning of a life cut short. I lit candles in the cathedral, praying for my mother's health as much as for the light to cast away the darkness that was taking over my spirit. I called her constantly, wanting to hear her calming voice and words. Once on stage, I felt empowered by the role she had so lovingly prepared me for, and I sang it with all the passion I felt.

Then, just a few months later, she was gone, and I lost forever my mother, my coach, my tutor, my biggest fan and source of light. My father and I walked around like two lost souls, each dealing with our loss in our own ways, our paths swerving in divergent directions without a pilot light to guide us.

Marcello's last words as Mimi's spirit took flight came back at me at the darkest of moments. It's what Lina would have also wished for us: "*Coraggio!/* Courage!"

Lina at piano recital, 1954

Lina and Louis on their wedding
day, Rome, 1949

Lina and Louis
in Rome, 1949

Lina, Louis, Gino and Donna in Paris, 1960s

Gino and Donna in Paris, 1960s

The Quilico family rehearsing at home in Toronto, 1990s

Lina in concert dress

ACT II
Louis: Mr. Rigoletto

Chapter 11
Loss

You were my Mimi, my Tosca, my Violetta, my Madama Butterfly. How could you leave me alone to fend for myself?

I spoke to Lina continuously in the first few months after her death, as I had done for the forty years we had been together, but now it was a one-way conversation that did nothing to alleviate my pain.

Lina, I feel lost without you and can't handle the loneliness.

Her loss ravaged my love of life. At times, I thought I felt her presence beside me, but I saw no one there. I cried whenever someone spoke of her. The children saw my pain and kept close to me whenever they could. Gino tried to cheer me up and stayed with me in my New York apartment when covering roles at the Met. I had an open invitation to his homes in Montreal and Florida, where we spent time together on his boat. I was inconsolable and unfocused, and when I tried to steer the boat, I crashed it against the dock behind his house. I felt debilitated, like an empty shell of what I had been, I easily became angry at everyone around me, especially at Gino, who kept his grief to himself. He was booked solid for the next three years and was continuously away from his family. I sensed that he and his wife, Kathy, were having problems.

You would have helped them settle their differences, but I don't know how to intervene. I feel so frustrated and helpless.

I continued my teaching and scheduled performances, but I shut myself off from the world when I was home. I walked around the house, staring at the framed photos that lined the corridors and spilled into the living room and our bedroom. Lina had been diligent in documenting the various phases of our journey as a family and as performers and kept scrapbooks of reviews and memorabilia. Through the pictures, I could relieve our early days in Rome, my first debuts, my performances next to some of the world's most respected singers—Renata Tebaldi, Joan Sutherland, Monserrat Caballé, Marilyn Horne, Leontyne Price, Mario del Monaco, Jon Vickers, Placido Domingo, José Carreras, Luciano Pavarotti—as well as the joint performances with Gino. It brought back to mind not only the applause and adulations. but the strict discipline instilled in me by Lina, who coached me note by note, verse by verse until the words and the music synched perfectly and naturally.

Once I joked to Lina that the way she had hung the photos in a neat row along the corridor reminded me of the Stations of the Cross in churches. Now, the characters in full costumes and makeup from my most memorable performances stared at me like phantoms from another life.

The walk down my Via Crucis eased some of my loneliness but also intensified my anguish. Even if my career continued as before, I feared it would all feel empty without Lina. I had always had her by my side as I rehearsed, travelled, performed. I had done it all for her.

I fell in love with her image on a poster in the window of the Archambault music store, and she was my muse from that moment on. When I finally met her, I felt clumsy and stupid next to her calm composure. After she first heard me sing, she didn't mince words: "You have the voice, but you need to study solfège," she told me. She later would say that she saw a diamond in me, but a rough one that needed polishing.

I had been picked to sing at the Most People Choir of Saint-Jacques Church as a schoolboy because of my strong bass voice. I sang my heart out, relying entirely on the beats of the choirmaster and my ear for music, for the notes on the music score sheets meant nothing to me, and I had no idea how the vocal cords worked.

Until I met Lina, all I knew was the mechanics and physics of bicycles learned at my father's bicycle shop. I knew that wheels, pedals, gears, and brakes had to work in unison to make the simple machine work efficiently. I learned how to make the necessary adjustments by watching my father, but I wasn't as good as he was because I didn't have the passion for it that he had. I did my job more-or-less adequately and stuck to the less demanding tasks: the oiling, the welding, driving the truck for pick-ups and deliveries and became a jack-of-all-trades—work that didn't feed my soul. I was happiest while singing but lacked the proper training. I sang in the truck as I drove and delivered the refurbished bicycles, and people would call my mother up and tell her, "We heard your son today pass by."

After meeting Lina, my choirmaster convinced her to give me my first music lessons. He paid her with the money I had refused for singing at church funerals and weddings. It had not felt right to be paid by the church for doing what I loved, especially as it was the church that made me believe that my voice was a gift from God. Once Lina and I became a couple, she also refused to be paid. Neither of us was ever motivated by money. We were motivated by the passion for our craft.

Lina, you were the guiding light I needed to follow my path.

She made me understand that my body was my only instrument, as the piano was for her—and the bicycle for my father. I had to keep my instrument tuned and handled with care and respect.

As an obedient and dutiful son, I left school at 14 so I could help the family. Ours was a large and demanding family, and I had an older brother and three sisters as well as a father who domineered over all of us, including our mother. The side of Dorchester Street in south-east Montreal where we lived was considered the red-light district of the city, where not much was expected of sons except to help support their struggling families and stay out of trouble. I worked for my room and board and had to ask my father for spending money. Even the prostitutes of the neighbourhood saw me as a goody-goody. When I was still at school, they would ask me to keep an eye on their sons and report back to them if they misbehaved. I was always happy to please, but then I caught the singing bug in the church choir. I later entered and won the Saint Jean Baptiste opera contest, despite being considered the most unlikely candidate. I wanted out of the bicycle business, but I didn't know how to go about it.

Chapter 12
The Quilicos

My family's history was not typical of the stories of other Italian immigrants in Montreal. The patriarch of our family and my grandfather, Antonio Quilico, was an engineer who, in 1909, came to Canada from Pavone, a quiet medieval town in the Marche region in Northern Italy. He had the choice of working in Egypt on the grandiose Suez Canal project, where he could have accumulated a small fortune. Many others in the Marche at the time were lured by the large salaries paid by the bourgeoisie in cosmopolitan Alexandria and then returned home to buy a property or start a small business.

He chose Canada instead, and took a job working for the Canadian Northern Railroad because of its stability and reputation as a safe and peaceful country. His wife had died when he was working on a project in Greece, and he had the future of his children—Luigi, Battista, and Antonietta—to consider, so he settled in Montreal.

Luigi was my father. The project for which my grandfather was hired was to cut a tunnel through Mount Royal—a mountain smack in the centre of our city that then separated the downtown train station from a residential part of town, the Town of Mount Royal.

My father, though a son of an engineer and educated man, did not aim for higher education for himself or any of his children. "Why waste your time in school?" he'd say. "I started my own business when I was

54

only thirteen." When he turned thirteen, his father had given him a bicycle and he charged a few cents for renting it out to a store delivery boy who could not afford to buy one. When other boys rushed to him with the same request, he realized that he could make his bicycle earn him as much as he was being paid in tips to work as a part-time busboy at the Ritz-Carlton Hotel without being bossed around by snotty waiters.

He knew enough math to figure out that with ten to twelve bicycles, he could become his own boss. He continued to work as a waiter at the hotel for a while, but then opened his small store to rent out bicycles. Eventually, people asked to buy bikes and have them serviced. This is how Bicycles Quilicot started. The addition of the letter "t" to his name on his store sign was his effort to erase his Italian identity; he never spoke Italian to us at home, even if he knew the language.

He not only sold and repaired bicycles, but then started a bicycle club and initiated the famous six-day bicycle races in the Montreal Forum. The cyclists raced for six full days, and the winner with the most laps won. This event created a lot of excitement and enthusiasm for the sport, and Montreal became the centre of the yearly six-day race attracting racers from the US and other parts of Canada. Father was wholly lost in the sport during the event and in the months leading up to it.

He also introduced an annual race from Quebec City to Montreal, covered extensively by the sportswriters of *Montréal Matin* and *The Montreal Star*. His name and his store became synonymous with bicycling in the sports world, and he became consumed by his business and the attention his various activities provided. Having achieved success and a degree of fame in his chosen field, he could not understand why his son would not want to share in it.

For my father, music was only useful in revving up spectators at the Forum and for dancing, as he was known to be a good dancer and a lady's man. Despite this, he fell in love with and married a very reserved and quiet girl, my mother, Jeanne Gravel. When he met her through his brother, she had plans to enter a convent and become a nun. One day, he showed up at the convent with a bouquet of roses and convinced her to leave and marry him. From the sisters, my mother had learned the art of bookbinding, music and how to cook. She never complained when Father was away nights at sporting events or meeting friends in nightclubs. She devoted her life to her children, cooked and baked as many as 125 *tourtieres*—meat pies—at a time. This tradition was not unusual in large French-Canadian families at the time, especially around Christmas. I could easily eat one of her pies in one sitting.

Father did not expect any of his children to achieve more than he had in life. The girls would marry and have children; his two sons would work in the family business. It was only when I became famous that he acknowledged what a gift my voice was, and that created a wall of resentment that lingered for years. It didn't help when he left my mother for a young woman he met at a bar, this after she had dedicated years to him and given him five children. My youngest sister Madeleine entered a convent for a while to get away from the chaos and strife the marriage breakup caused the family.

Chapter 13
Finding my Voice

It was Lina that pulled me away from the years of subjugation I had suffered under my father's autocratic demands. I worked for over ten years at the bicycle store without any pay. His only dream for me was to be his assistant, and he considered my wish to pursue a singing career a silly childish fantasy. I envied Lina, whose parents encouraged her to pursue her passion for the piano. I was amazed that they allowed her to travel alone to Paris to study under a famous pianist, Cortot, of whom I had never heard.

My friend the tenor André Turp encouraged me to take lessons with Frank A. Rowe, who had also taught Maureen Forrester. When Rowe agreed to teach me, I started thinking of myself as a serious student of opera. With the Saint Jean Baptiste competition, I also won a prize to study in Italy. I didn't know how I'd be able to do it without financial assistance. My father half-heartedly gave me $450, not enough to get me there or pay for a place to live in Rome. When I learned that Lina's parents had accompanied her to New York on her way to Paris, I followed them and made the drastic decision to work on a freight ship as a way to get to Rome. Only my mother and my younger sister Madeleine came to bid me goodbye at the train station. I asked them why they were crying. My mother answered, "I think we're losing you." I also became very emotional and started to cry. I was scared and sad to be leaving my mother for an unknown destination.

My grandfather and father spoke multiple languages, but I had never learned to speak Italian. For me, Rome was as far away as Mars, and I had no idea what I would find there. I only knew that Italy was the best place to study opera. I had only one address for a place to sleep—a *pensione*—and the name of the famous baritone Riccardo Straccieri and a couple of other potential teachers scribbled on a piece of paper. Would they really help me? "You'll find someone else if they won't," Lina had assured me. "Italy is full of singing teachers." It had all seemed so easy and possible to Lina, and because she made me believe in myself, I found the courage to break away from my father's influence and travel across an ocean. But I also feared I'd lose her to Paris. I had used the little extra money I had to buy her a ring and propose to her in Central Park before leaving on our separate journeys.

That ring was the best investment I ever made, Lina, and after you accepted it, I felt ready to face whatever challenge awaited me.

I fed 149 cows, one bull, and 18 chickens, and cleaned their stalls in return for my transatlantic fare. I never forgot that crossing.

On my arrival in Rome, a *carabinieri* accompanied me to the *pensione* not far from the station. The ladies of the night I saw walking up and down the street reminded me of my friends' mothers I had known as a schoolboy in Montreal. Their presence and the run-down *pensione* didn't bother me. I stayed there three days, after which time I went to a convent where I slept on a mattress on the floor. I found kindness and a sense of renewal everywhere in Rome, a city that had experienced the bombings and destructions of World War II and wanted desperately to spring back to life, both economically and culturally. The convent sisters arranged for me to meet Riccardo Stracciari, who took me on as a student. When Lina joined me in Rome a few months and we were married, she insisted we look for better accommodations. I'll never forget what a blessing Signora Valeri and her boarding house were. Had it not been for her generosity, we would have starved.

Our stay in Rome turned out to be an intense year of study and discovery. Though a good singer himself, Stracciari spent too much time talking about himself and his past glories, and I quit after three lessons. We searched Rome for the best singing teachers for me and piano teachers for Lina. She studied with famed pianist and conductor Carlo Zecchi;

I, with Maria Teresa Pediconi, who quickly enrolled me at the renowned Accademia di Santa Cecilia. As eager as I was to learn as much about singing as possible, Lina accompanied me to my lessons and then also took some lessons from Pediconi. Lina asked many questions, so much so that she annoyed Pediconi, who asked me to come alone. But Lina soon made me realize that with Pediconi, I was losing my voice rather than opening it, and we searched elsewhere. It turned out to be the best decision at that point.

We found Walter Brunelli, a tenor, who immediately told me to stop trying to sing like a tenor, that my voice was that of a pure baritone. In only two lessons with him, I reached a high C while remaining a baritone. With Signora Pediconi, my highest tone had been an F. My progress from then on was phenomenal. But our money could not last beyond that first year. We had applied for but did not receive any grants from the Quebec government, although we met other less talented singers and musicians from Quebec studying in Rome with government grants.

On our return to Montreal, Lina entered me in the CBC 1953 Futures étoiles competition. I won and then applied for a scholarship at the Mannes Institute of Music in New York City to study with Martial Singher, the leading baritone at the Met. "Let's go," she said, even though she had to leave her own studies and was pregnant with our daughter, Donna.

My enthusiasm to study and improve myself was at its peak, even though I had to work at all types of odd jobs to feed our growing family. A job as a night elevator operator at the Statler Hotel suited me best for a while as it freed me up during the day to attend classes at the Institute. Despite living in Jackson Heights, New York, I still had to respect my Futures étoiles contract in Quebec and sing 26 radio shows and 42 concerts in major cities in the province. I juggled the back and forth between Jackson Heights and Montreal, my job at the hotel, and my classes at the Institute.

After one of those concerts in Montreal, Lina taught me a lesson in humility. Music critic Jean Vallerand wrote in *Le Devoir* that, though I had been gifted with a good voice, my musicianship was very poor. Rather than respond with indignation as I was tempted to do, Lina insisted I reflect on the criticism and start working seriously on my musicianship. She then found the time to teach me some *solfeggio*, a system used in music conservatories worldwide to read every note in the beat as written on a music score. It was like learning the ABCs of music. The next time I met Vallerand, I shook his hand and thanked him for his comments, which surprised and pleased him immensely.

After Lina's parents bought a house in Flushing Meadows, our life became less stressful, and I began to concentrate solely on my singing.

The year 1955 turned out to be a glorious one! While Lina was pregnant with our second child, she entered my name for the Metropolitan Opera on Air. I was scared. "Just try!" she told me, "It's the only way you'll know if you're good enough." It would be a challenging exercise with a radio audition against twenty-two male singers and twenty-two female singers. The eleven chosen would then sing on the Met stage. I was elated to be one of the eleven, and it was a thrill I'll never forget.

As I walked onto the Met stage for the first audition, I was well aware that I, an unknown from Quebec, who spoke broken English and bad Italian and had little musical training, had the least chance of winning. Knowing that it was the same stage where Caruso had sung made my knees tremble. Around my neck, I wore the medallion with the head of a wolf that Lina had bought me in Rome. "*In bocca al lupo* / Go in the mouth of the wolf"—the Italian equivalent of "Break a leg!" At Lina's suggestion, I chose to sing in French, "*Avant de quitter ces lieux*," from Faust. I sang live with the ABC orchestra conducted by Max Rudolf.

Lina and I were ecstatic when after the first round, I was one of four finalists. They would announce the winner at the end of the dress rehearsal for the final concert on air. When they called my name at the end as the winner, I hyperventilated.

"Go outside for some air," Lina told me. She was almost nine months pregnant and resting on a chair outside the auditorium. Family members had not been allowed in. I ran out of the ABC building even though it was drizzling and found myself on 42nd Street and Broadway, lying on a bench with two policemen attending to me. I had fainted from the pent-up nerves and excitement. "Call an ambulance," I heard one of them say. I got up, my pant legs wet and muddy from water splashed by passing cars, and ran back as fast as I could for the final performance. The following day I saw my name for the first time in *The New Yorker*.

Two weeks later, Gino was born—a further promise of new life! The contest was a major stepping stone among many obstacles I faced as I built my career. I felt that after that challenge, I could overcome anything. Still, I also understood that, without years of musical training, I had to master my own voice on my own terms, not by following some theoretical technique out of a book. Lina sensed my fears and urged me to get in touch with my body and recognize that I could not control the voice without controlling the mind; this still needed some work.

I found an agent, Thea Dispeker. She booked me for musical comedies in New York and a contract with the American Opera Society. When she announced that she had secured a contract for me to sing in San Francisco for Kurt Herbert Adler for the entire opera season, I panicked. The Austrian American conductor and director had transformed the San Francisco Opera into one of the leading opera companies in America. Expectations would be very high, and I was still so green. I'd be performing next to Jussi Bjorling, Dorothy Kristen, and other big names in opera at the time. It was also intimidating knowing that my roles had been meant for Martial Singher, my old teacher, who turned them down because of a conflict in his schedule. On top of that, I'd have to learn five different operas in five months and open with *Manon Lescaut*. I found Puccini more challenging to sing than Verdi because of how the rhythms change repeatedly in his music, and it would be the first time I'd be singing in such a large concert hall. In other words, I found as many excuses as possible to convince myself that I was aiming too high, too soon.

Lina tried to reassure me that she would work hard to teach me the scores. What scared me most was that although I had learned much about singing, I still didn' really understand how my voice box produced the right sounds, and without this awareness, I felt I could not be in total control of my voice.

Early one morning, I shut myself in my studio, stood five or six feet away from a wall, with eyes closed, and sang against the wall uninterrupted for hours, sometimes as loudly as if on stage, sometimes just in a whisper. I wanted to hear my voice bounce back from the wall to understand how the voice came out of my body and how it sounded. I did this until I felt a kind of communication between the wall and my mind. I fell into a trance and never even heard Lina opening the door from time to time to check on me. I stood in front of that wall for eight hours, transporting myself into a third dimension, into a dream world, until I started to shake like a leaf in Lina's arms.

I did this several times in the next weeks at varying distances from the wall and at different tonalities to feel the relationship between my vocal cords and my breath, to figure out how approach the breath, the space, and to find the concentration needed for vocal production. I did it until I fully felt the opening of my head, my breath, and my throat, going exactly where it belonged. Finally, the intangible quality of my voice became more tangible and thus more easily wielded and less likely to fail me. I had a semi-spiritual experience in front of that wall in Flushing Meadows when I heard my voice echoed back. I wanted to shatter that wall with my voice—a wall built up by years of deep-felt insecurities.

"Do or die!" You dared me, Lina, and I took the challenge.

Still, the road was not suddenly strewn with rose petals. I was still considered an up-and-coming baritone and had to fight to be taken seriously and recognized. Before going to San Francisco, I sang in two musical shows, *Paint your Wagon* and *Rose-Marie,* both about miners, one set in Gold Rush-era California, the other in the Canadian Rockies. I had to learn how to dance, which was even more difficult for me than learning *solfeggio,* and the experience made me feel like a wild horse in a saloon.

In my first rehearsal in San Francisco, I was suffering from bronchitis, and I sang badly. The conductor, Oliviero de Fabritis, an Italian, didn't think I could pull it off and asked Adler to replace me, but fortunately, Adler stood up for me. Whether from bronchitis or nerves, the night before my debut, I lost my voice. Lina made me drink two bottles of warmed red wine. I went to bed drunk but giddy and relaxed. The morning after, I could hardly walk, but when I opened my mouth, my voice was back.

Before going on stage, I paced nervously. Bjorling, also pacing backstage, noticed my nervousness. He told me not to worry so much because the public didn't expect anything from me. "They are here to listen to me, not you. You are a young artist. If you do well, they will be very happy; if you do not do well, they will not remember you." Rather than be offended by his words, they eased my anxiety slightly.

After the performance, the conductor, who also had not expected much from me, came backstage and congratulated me, "*Complimenti*, I was wrong. I'm happy Adler kept you in the opera. You do have a voice."

The following day, the local opera critic wrote, "Verdian baritones are not born every day; we have one, let's cherish him—Louis Quilico."

We often speak of the 50s, 60s, and 70s as the golden age of singers with great divas Maria Callas, Renata Tebaldi, Joan Sutherland, Beverly

Sills, and Leontyne Price and the celebrated Leonard Warren, Mario del Monaco, Boris Christoff, and Jussi Bjorling. I met and watched them all in San Francisco. I studied how they took a breath and their posture as they sang the high notes. Then I shared my observations with Lina, who gave me further instructions. At first, I felt ridiculous exaggerating my movements on stage, but she insisted I exaggerate even more. She pushed and pushed and often got mad at me, but in the end, her coaching made me a better artist.

In the spring of 1956, I found myself at the City Opera singing in *La Traviata* with Beverly Sills, who looked like an angel to me with her long red hair. Singing at City Opera in those early years was frightening because there was no prompter and you were really on your own on stage. But it turned out to be the best learning experience, and so unbelievable to sing on stage next to a star like Beverly Sills.

I was still underpaid, and despite my artistic successes, I could not afford to live in New York and support a family of four My father convinced me to return to the bicycle shop in Montreal. It didn't take me long to realize that working for my father was not tenable. Besides the low salary, our arguments became more and more hostile. I was no longer the good-natured boy who obeyed him and had no worries about money. I had two children to feed, tuxedos and evening clothes for our concerts to buy, singing coaches to pay, and occasionally travel expenses to cover when I was invited to sing elsewhere. But I had no training other than singing and fixing bicycles. Against Lina's wishes, I thought I could run my own bicycle business.

Lina, now that you're gone, all the fears I faced those first years are haunting me again.

The resentment I felt towards my father, my senseless attempt to become a business owner and compete with him, the sense of failure when my business went bankrupt, and especially the painful silence that followed between my father and me, all of it still gnaws at me.

I worked so hard to prove him wrong and to prove you right, Lina!

Chapter 14
A Career

After Lina left me, the framed images on the walls and photo albums became my only solace and the only tangible reminders that I had succeeded. Honours and accolades followed over the years, but not without constant struggle, work, and pain. Singing opera requires years of discipline and commitment, just like ballet, painting, or elite sports, and only a few make it to the top. Often luck also plays a part—being in the right place and at the right time.

Not being wealthy was a big stumbling block for me. As an emerging singer I was not well paid, and I did not have a rich family to back me up. Such was the reason for my first refusal to sing at Covent Gardens. Sir David Webster offered me a contract in the late 50s, while I was still struggling with my business in Montreal, but I could not accept it because I knew that the sixty pounds a week they were offering was not enough to support a family in London. Frustrated and upset, I tore up the contract. Sir Webster was insulted that I would refuse such a prestigious offer and sent back a stern reply, "You are never going to sing at Covent Garden." But lady luck was on my side, or at least my voice was.

I sang in Spoleto, Italy, that same summer in *Il Duca D'Alba*, produced by Luchino Visconti, then famous for his Italian film productions. Sir Webster happened to be there and heard me sing, and he congratulated me on the quality of my voice, "Rich, powerful, dramatic," he said. He had discovered Canadian singers like Richard Verreau, André Turp, Robert Savoie, Joseph Rouleau, and had picked out such artists as Joan Sutherland and Jon Vickers. He forgot his earlier threat and invited me to sing in *La Traviata* with Joan Sutherland. I accepted.

It turned out that Joan and the Maestro, Nello Santi, were not on good terms and played tricks on each other during rehearsals, such as not respecting each other's music beat. I was also told to expect boos since I had replaced one of the audience's favourite baritones who had been fired. The evening of my debut, I was a pack of nerves and begged Joan to follow the beat of the conductor, or I'd have problems following him. Of course, Joan was a true professional, and all went well. The public appreciated my performance, and she later apologized for causing me such nerves at my debut. It took a bit of maneuvering by my agent, but finally, Sir Webster offered me a contract for ninety pounds a week. I declared bankruptcy and moved the family to London.

I had some outstanding performances at Covent Gardens. I especially appreciated the English audience, which was always warm and honest in their applauses. I had my most memorable and unforgettable performance there with *Lucia di Lammermoor* with Joan Sutherland. After singing the sextet, the public went wild and kept on screaming *bis, bis.* In the constitution of Covent Gardens, performers are not allowed to *bis*, so everyone, from the conductor to Joan, just stood there not knowing what to do. Then the conductor gave the signal and we all started again. The nearly 500 spectators brought the house down with the biggest applause ever; they even waited for us for our autographs on street afterwards. It was only the second *bis* in the history of Covent Gardens. The first one was for Maria Callas and Ebe Stignani, a dramatic mezzo-soprano, after their duet in *Norma*.

While in London, I had the good fortune to meet the Russian Maestro Melik Tschaiev when he conducted Tchaikovsky's *The Queen of Spades* at Covent Garden in 1960 and he invited me to Russia. The opera is based on a novella by the great Russian writer Alexander Pushkin and is set in St. Petersburg. The city was renamed Leningrad during the communist period. I could not wait to sing at the famous Bolshoi Theatre in Moscow and the Kiov Theatre in Leningrad. It was at the Kiov Theatre, formerly the Mariinsky Theatre, that the opera premiered in 1890. I was the first opera singer invited to Russia as a private guest since the Revolution. Others had travelled there as part of cultural exchanges, but these took years to arrange. Touring Russia and singing at the two theatres turned out to be more than just a cultural experience for me. I felt a real affinity with the Russian spirit. Italian art and architecture had greatly influenced Russian culture during the time of Peter the Great, who envisioned Saint Petersburg as a Venice in the Baltic. Both the Bolshoi and the Mariinsky theatres were designed by a Russian architect of Italian origin, Alberto Cavos, under the direction of Italian Carlo Rossi. The colours and horseshoe shape of the Bolshoi reminded me of an old Italian opera house.

One day after rehearsal of *Falstaff* sung in Russian, I sat in the theatre to reflect on the incongruity of singing an Italian opera in Russian in a Russian theatre designed by an Italian. I closed my eyes to savour the experience. After a while, I forgot I was in a country as different and as far away as Russia. The theatre felt like my natural home. It's where I was always destined to be. "Thank you, God," I whispered. I felt a great sense of unity with a higher presence as if I were in a church speaking directly to God. It was a revelation. I thought this is how the children of Fatima or Lourdes must have felt. My revelation was not a vision but the sensation that my body was elevated to another dimension, and I felt closer to God than ever before. I only shared the experience with Lina and Gino, afraid that anyone else would find me delusional for even thinking I'd spoken to God in communist Russia of all places!

I made a poor decision when, in 1962, I decided to leave London for Paris. Though one of the greatest opera houses I have ever sang in, Covent Garden at the time was also rife with petty jealousies and politics and offered meager monetary rewards. Other artists, better off than me financially, were happy to sing there for the prestige, but I could not afford such luxury, and the Paris Opera offered me better pay and working conditions. What I had not considered was the red tape I found in Paris as a foreign performer. The union would not allow me to do recordings there, whereas in England as a Canadian, there were no such restrictions. It would have been possible at the time to accept to sing in Paris and still maintain my contract in London, but when young and inexperienced, one makes rash decisions without considering the consequences.

My role in Paris of the Marquis de Posa in *Don Carlos* is the one that many people still remember. The beauty of the music moves me every time. I sang at the premiere, which had a special significance for the Paris

Opera, because Giuseppe Verdi wrote *Don Carlos* specifically for the house, but it had not been performed in Paris since a production at the Théâtre Impérial de l'Opéra in 1867. It's a grand opera from a French-language libretto with Verdi's greatest music, but also a difficult one to produce because its lengthy five acts make it hard to cut down without compromising the drama.

It also became significant for me because it's the first opera in which my children saw me sing, and Lina told me they sat transfixed for the full duration of the performance. When they came backstage, I saw tears in Gino's eyes. I asked him what he didn't like about the opera. He replied, "I loved it, but Daddy, don't sing it again. I hate to see people kill you."

In the middle of one of the twenty-four performances of *Don Carlos*, I received a telegram that my mother had died in Montreal. I had to go on and sing with passion and pain. Lina, in the audience with a family friend, told me that they both cried with me at the last scene. They both felt a deep emotion and so did my fans, some of whom came backstage to tell me how they had been moved by my singing. I flew home for the funeral the day after and returned within a few days to resume performances.

I received praise from over forty different newspapers all over Europe and two terrible reviews from the French publications, *Opera* and *Entracte*. One critic, a certain Mancini, completely dismissed me and wrote, "He is not even an opera singer." They later told me that Mancini only gave good reviews to those that subscribed to his magazines. I met him a few months later, introduced myself, and called him an SOB to his face.

I became frustrated in Paris. They have one of the most beautiful and opulent opera houses in the world, but their constitution made it difficult for non-French artists. They insisted I sing *Rigoletto* in French. Whenever I sang it in Italian, I'd get fifteen and eighteen curtain calls, but the director kept repeating that it was a French opera house. Language was important for their national image. Because of my insistence on singing only in the original Italian, they gave me only nine performances of *Rigoletto* in four years, though the opera was in the repertoire repeatedly. I was well paid, but I felt with all these restrictions, I was not developing artistically in Paris.

Rome had a special place in our hearts, and we decided to make it our home. I would sing there as a free agent. Living there was less expensive than anywhere in Europe, yet the quality of life and *joie de vivre* was unparalleled in the late 60s. I sang in all the great European opera houses while living in Rome, but never got to sing at La Scala. It is one of my great regrets. Both times that I was invited to sing there, some unfortunate incident or scheduling conflict prevented it from happening. Then we left Rome unexpectedly, and I cut ties with Europe after we moved to New York and then Toronto. The decision to leave Europe for North America was not an easy one, but both Lina and I and the rest of the family longed for more stability, and it turned out to be the right decision for me.

The Canadian opera world welcomed me with open arms. I was honoured to be invited to sing in a production of *Otello* conducted by the incomparable Zubin Mehta, alongside Jon Vickers for Expo 1967, a world exhibition in Montreal that drew millions of people from around the globe and gave Canadians a sense of pride and identity.

My biggest successes were had at the Metropolitan Opera, where I had a life contract, but my pride almost blocked me from getting there. Back in 1955, after having won the Metropolitan Opera on Air audition, the general manager of the Met, Mr. Rudolf Bing—still only a Mr. then, he only to became a Sir later—had offered me a contract. I turned it down because it was just a chorus role with little pay. Both Lina and I wanted more. After my early successes, I continued auditioning for roles at the Met but was rejected time and time again. I became very bitter and simply stopped auditioning for Bing.

In 1960, while singing at Covent Garden, Mr. Bing's scout asked me to audition for him in Milan. Still smarting from the rejections, I answered that if Mr. Bing wanted to hear me, he could find me in London. Highly insulted, he replied that as long as he was manager at the Met I'd never sing there. He kept his word, and I mine. I never auditioned for him again. But general managers come and go, so when Schuyler Chapin replaced Rudolf Bing, it was only a matter of time before I found myself in the right place at the right time, just as it had been with Covent Garden.

The day after a successful performance of *The Trojans* in Boston in 1972, I was at the airport for a flight to Toronto. I caught sight of Sir Colin Davis, conductor of the London Symphony Orchestra, walking towards the same gate. The plane had a stop-over in New York and he was on his way there to conduct *Pelléas et Mélisande* at the Met. I told him that it was one of my favourite operas and asked if they were rehearsing for the production. The cast was full and rehearsals completed, he replied, and we just said our goodbyes. The next afternoon, while I was in Toronto teaching, I received an urgent call from my agent, Ellen

Wood, "Would you want to make your debut at the Met on Thursday in the role of Galaud?" I thought about it for an hour or so and said yes, even though Lina thought I was a little crazy because I was totally unprepared. After my class I rushed home, took the score, and studied it with Lina at the piano. I flew to New York the morning after, was fitted for costumes, and rehearsed all day. Sir Rudolf Bing walked in during the rehearsal and we shook hands but he left without exchanging any words. They offered me a contract that lasted 24 years—they were best years of my career.

Of my first performance in *Otello* in 1972, the New York Post critic wrote, "Louis Quilico blessed with a gorgeous voice sang his first Met Iago… and showed the splendor of his voice."

A year later, in *Faust*, I impressed the very demanding music critic from *The New York Times*. "Singing Valentine for the first time at the Met was Louis Quilico. Best of all, Mr. Quilico sang in a golden-age manner, too, making easily the finest vocal impression of the night"

While at the Met, I became a household name in Canadian opera houses as well. For a CBC telecast of *Macbeth* in November 1973, Eric Mclean of the *Montreal Star* described my voice this way, "His is the most powerful voice Canada has produced."

I sang *Aida* in front of Canada's Prime Minister Pierre Elliott Trudeau, after which *The Globe and Mail* wrote, "Louis Quilico…. seemed to be in the top of his great vocal form, for not only was his voice robustly beautiful, but it was also a superb interpretive instrument, that conveyed tenderness and remorse as effectively as it communicated anger and stormy passion."

In 1974, I was accorded the highest honour for a performer in Canada, Companion of the Order of Canada, awarded by Governor General Jules Leger. I cultivated a worldwide reputation as a classic Verdian baritone and none other than Luciano Pavarotti confirmed it. He wrote about me, "I have sung over a hundred performances with Louis Quilico, more than sixty of them at the Met, and I think that Louis has one of the few real and unique Verdi baritone voices that still exist. He is also very human." Lina and I enjoyed the greatest dinner parties with him.

Oh, Lina, I cannot fathom attending parties without you! Those glorious years are over for me.

I only bothered to look through the album of reviews that Lina had religiously kept over the years once she left me and I was alone in the house. I perused it to remind myself of what we had all accomplished together as a family.

While I continued my journey in North America, Gino also found his way into the world of opera. He gives the outward impression that everything is easy for him, yet I saw how hard he worked to master his craft and advance on his own merit. Our two voices are very different and so is our physicality. We have always understood our limitations and what roles we do best. I stopped accepting the role of Escamillo when I started gaining weight, and he has remained in the lighter lyrical baritone ranges of French operas. He has become an artist in his own right, and I have experienced the greatest satisfaction singing next to him.

He had his first taste of the stage as a four-year-old playing Madama Buttefly's son, Trouble, and showed his stubborn nature even then. He rehearsed his silent part well, but when it came time to appear on stage in the performance, he refused to go on, saying he thought he had done his job already.

There are not many operas with two important baritone parts, and we have both gladly accepted minor roles in order to sing together. He first sang next to me at the start of his career in Rigoletto as Marullo. I sensed his nervousness, but he was brave enough to go on stage, and he didn't disappoint me. We sang twice together for the Canadian Opera Company, he in the role of Paolo to my Simon Boccanegra, and I as Leporello to his Don Giovanni. In 1982, we sang together at a Command Performance for Queen Elizabeth II on the occasion of the repatriation of the Canadian Constitution. Finally, in 1987, we were honored with the first father and son performance at the Met in *Manon Lescaut*—an event highly covered in the news and especially significant for both of us. They re-invited us both for *The Barber of Seville*, two years later, with Marilyn Horne, who sang her last performance as Rosina. We never overshadowed but instead always complemented each other.

I have been fully supportive of Gino but have also expected the best from him. It was sheer determination that brought me to sing the most difficult and demanding roles under the most important conductors in the world. The many praises and honours I received throughout the years helped me develop the confidence to speak my mind with conductors if I disagreed with them. I tried to instill the same principles of honesty in my son and to encourage him to, first and foremost, never compromise his artistic integrity.

Our years of struggles had finally paid off when, in our home in Toronto, Lina and I found the perfect balance of work, travel, family, teaching. Grateful, Lina wanted to give something back, and I encouraged her in her *Water for Africa* project and travelled to Africa with her. We were more together than ever, and almost breathed as one. Sharing teaching at the Faculty of Music at the University of Toronto, gave both of us great joy. Together through our own fundamental singing rules and principles, we helped launch the careers of many young and talented singers, including Paul Frey, Thomas Goerz, Mark Pedrotti, John Fanning, Gary Relyea, as well as our son, Gino, to name but a few. Without the formal musical background that such a position usually demands, I taught as I sang, from the gut, the heart, and from life experiences.

The teaching became a blessing after a freak accident on a plane caused damage to my knee, making air travel difficult. I had suffered from knee pain for years, caused by some arthritis and the extra weight I had gained over time. A knee operation proved unsuccessful, but I still managed to control the pain with medication. I learned I could not walk long distances or stand for long periods, but I never had to curtail my travel or miss a performance.

In 1980 on a flight from London, I was dozing with one leg extended into the aisle when a run-away beverage cart hit my leg, pinning it to the metal armrest and breaking a bone in my already compromised knee. The pain was excruciating, and so was the later realization that I had lost some of my agility. The accident cost me some important roles overseas, even if my voice had not suffered any damage.

As I became more and more despondent after Lina's death, my knee pain became more acute. I sat for hours looking at my home library filled with impressive books on great composers and the history of music and opera. I had not read one of those books because Lina had read them for me, imparting the valuable knowledge to me as she went. Each day without her made her absence a reality I could not change. My sense of gloom deepened as I retraced our journey. I couldn't get the smell of those animal stalls from the freight ship on my way to Rome out of my mind!

Lina, I'm so alone.

Chapter 15
Rigoletto

Though I suffered silently inside, my professionalism and love of the stage never wavered. It was the only pleasure I had left. In my first performance of *Rigoletto* after Lina's death, the *Montreal Gazette* critic wrote, "Louis Quilico portrayed Rigoletto with dramatic strength. His rich voice brought volume and depth to this role. The quality of the singing was above that of everyone else."

> *I cinched it again, Lina. After all, I'm not known as Mr. Rigoletto for nothing.*

My most amazing reviews were of my performances as Rigoletto, and I read and reread them all when alone with my thoughts. One that made me rethink the opera and its significance in my life appeared in *The New York Times* after a performance at the Met with Luciano Pavarotti.

> Though Luciano Pavarotti as the Duke may attract the most attention, Louis Quilico as Rigoletto, was at the centre of the drama; His passions and fears could be heard in his voice as well as seen in his face and body, His "La ra, la ra, la ra" seemed sobbed out by a jester who has lived too long and has seen too much. (Dec. 11, 1981)

Rigoletto is a tragic and complex character who lives a life of evil and deceit as a court jester. The only light of his life is his love for his daughter Gilda, whom he so jealously tries to protect from the life he, himself, perpetuates. Rigoletto is cursed by his physical deformity. He is called a monster by those around him at court, both because of his appearance as his acid tongue and evil manipulations. Acting like a clown, he entertains his master, the Duke, while sparing nothing to satisfy the Duke's every licentious whim.

Rigoletto is aware of the tragic nature of his being. He sings, "I rage at my monstrous form, my cap and bells! To be permitted nothing but to laugh! I'm denied that common human right, to weep."

This is the character that, more than any others, brought out my strongest emotions on stage and who lingered the longest after each performance. He spoke to me as an artist and performer as well as a father. We put on our masks like jesters to play-act our different roles while hiding the personal pain we feel inside. I connected to his loneliness, despair, and ultimate pain at the fate of his daughter Gilda as I reflected on the troubled life of my own daughter Donna.

Rigoletto shelters Gilda so much that she is entirely unprepared to weed out even the most obvious of dangers that cross her path. She is an overprotected child with no identity or sense of where she belongs. She asks her father, "What country do I come from?" She has been given much love but little life skills to detect the evil around her. A naïve, innocent young woman, she succumbs to the advances of the deceitful and licentious Duke, her father's patron, who ultimately causes her death.

I own the role of Rigoletto and have sung it over five hundred times, more than one thousand if we count the dress rehearsals. I have become Mr. Rigoletto, and at the time of Lina's death at sixty-seven years of age, I questioned not only how long I could maintain the strength the role demands, but also how much we had sacrificed for the sake of my art, and, as a father, whether I had failed in my duties towards my own family, especially Donna.

As I perused the framed reviews, the magazine articles and a book written about my family, I became aware that throughout the years, we had highlighted my career and Gino's. My audience must have thought that I did not have a daughter, a beautiful daughter who loved ballet and all forms of dancing and was and still remains a free spirit.

Donna started down a similar artistic path as Gino but she was not as consumed by the desire to achieve the heights of fame. Her pregnancy at age 15 certainly derailed her studies for a time. Though we offered to take care of David for her while studying in Montreal at Les Grand Ballets Canadiens, she could not bear the long absences from her son and quit the ballet.

Lina, should we have given her dancing more attention? Were we too indulgent with her because she was a girl?

Lina and I were never carried away by the social and often scandalous life that obsesses many musicians. We were never led astray by or desired illicit sexual relationships with others. Our only addiction was opera and all that it entails: study, practice, rehearsals, performances, travel. If anything, pride was my folly. The children were left in the good hands of Lina's mother when we couldn't take them with us. But even when at home, always overly preoccupied with the next concert, I was an absent father. As the children grew up, most of the attention was placed first on my career, then after his teen years, on Gino's. We were never as disciplined with Donna and her artistic goals. Did our success impose unrealistic expectations on her and feelings of resentments at her missed opportunities? These questions had never occurred to me while Lina was at my side, but suddenly I felt, if not guilt, a heaviness of heart each time I played so fully the role of Rigoletto.

Like Gilda, Donna made some unwise choices in men. Her hurried first marriage as a pregnant teen was held in Las Vegas and was as quickly annulled when her husband renounced their son David. Her second husband, Franco, was no better than a small-time crook and exploited the generosity of our family while mistreating her. He cheated and embezzled to pay for his gambling and spent evenings at bars. They had a daughter, Natasha, whom we embraced, and Lina had a second story built onto our house so we could take care of Donna and her family. Gino was frequently angered by Franco's abusive behaviour, his drinking, his gambling, and his constant siphoning of money from us. It was finally Gino who threw Franco out of the house and the family then decided to leave the country. After all the help we had given him, Franco seemed to have done this out of spite for our family. Lina and I were devastated by their move, not knowing how Franco would be able to provide for Donna and her children, and how the move would affect David's schooling. They would be living with Franco's parents, as he had no job prospects there. Given these uncertainties, the whole family, including Donna, decided it would be best for David to remain in Canada with us. I remembered my mother's words to me when I went to Rome as Donna herself left, "I think we're losing you," but how it must have hurt Donna to leave her beloved child behind!

Like many adolescents, David suffered some angst as a teen. He looked up to Gino who was more of a big brother than an uncle for him.. He had only known our home and he had our name, Quilico, after his biological father had renounced him. He must have often missed his mother and yearned to know his real father. Did he ever wonder, who is my real mother, my real father?

Donna's sense of identity must also have been distorted by never having the security of a home of her own as a married woman. She returned to Toronto when Lina was diagnosed with cancer, but was still struggling in her relationship with her husband and was maybe wounded beyond repair. Rigoletto's final cry at the death of his daughter and the breakup of the only family he had known, haunts me. It haunts me every time I sing it. "Oh, my daughter! No, you must not leave me, do not die. If you go away, I shall be alone! Do not die, or I shall die beside you."

Living alone with my thoughts and falling into a deep depression, I also started thinking of my mortality, but more than my physical death, I feared that the best time of my life was behind me and that as an artist, I was slowly passing away.

Lina, I need you more than ever.

Chapter 16
A New Pianist

Only months after Lina left me, I was surprised to see young women performers, half my age, younger than Gino and Donna, buzz around me, vying for my attention. I knew that Lina might be troubled by their presence.

Lina, it doesn't make me happy, only confused and uncomfortable.

While she was alive, I refused to kiss women on the mouth out of respect for her in my performances. We never questioned each other's fidelity even as we saw cheating and betrayals all around us. Now the thought of intimacy with anyone else terrified me. Just having young women around me felt like being unfaithful to her memory, and it didn't flatter me.

Do you understand the void you left in my life, Lina?

When you are in love for so long with one person, everything is contained in that one person: your youth, your dreams, the days of hunger, the birth of your children, the exaltation of the first big role, the shared applause, your expectations for the future. You can access the thrill of those moments every time you hold each other's hand, make love to each other.

I cannot put my arms around your memory, around a shadow that I feel but do not see.

You need a real body to feel the lost sensation of youth.

Lina, I miss you.

I'm confident she understood but didn't like it one bit seeing the young things flirt with me, trying to catch my attention, and neither did the children, who were busy with their own lives and understood loneliness far less than I did.

I feared Gino's sarcasm when it came to these young women. Donna and David also seemed concerned by seeing me surrounded by the young hopefuls so soon after Lina's passing. "What if he lets himself be tempted by someone our age?" They must have asked each other. I could read concern in their eyes while also hurting and missing their mother and grandmother. They never asked me questions, but I felt their uneasiness around me as if this were my fault. A wall of silence slowly rose around us, and I was helpless in breaking it down

A few months after Lina's death, life had taken on a monotonous pattern. I respected all my scheduled performances but had lost any enthusiasm for soliciting new ones. I lived alone with David in a huge home built for an extended family that seen both happy and sad moments but had always been full of laughter and music. Gino and I went on tour to Japan together with the Metropolitan Opera. I was covering *Un Ballo in Maschera* and Gino was singing Escamillo in *Carmen* with Jose Carreras. Performances brought us together for a while, but without Lina around to act as a go-between, I sensed that our differences in personality were more apparent. The cockiness and self-assurance that had once made me smile now irked me. I had always held my own with directors and even given them a piece of my mind when called for, but always respectfully, while he was too quick to burn his bridges. In magazines, they called him the bad boy of opera, and in one, he posed sitting on his motorcycle, his bare arms tattooed with the image of a wolf and the words, "*In bocca al lupo.*" Lina had asked me to buy him a medallion with those words in Milan when I surprised him for his debut there. The three of us wore similar medallions around our necks for all our performances, but seeing a tattoo of it on his arms made me cringe. Had Lina and I spent years training him for classical opera so he could now sing looking like a member of a motorcycle gang?

David had also tried singing but soon came to his own realization that he did not want to pursue it as a career, and we never pressed him, just as we had never pressed Gino. The desire for this type of life must come from deep in your guts. If not, even if very talented, you sink under its pressures. I was happy that David still wanted to build a career around music. He focused on composing and studied diligently at York University.

One late afternoon, one of David's music teachers, a pianist appeared at our home to give him an assignment. It was unusual for a teacher to do this and if it was ruse to meet me, it worked. I was home; we were introduced and talked music till 3:00 a.m.

A new pianist entered my life and, in many ways, changed it!

I could feel the children's relief when I started a relationship with her—someone younger than me by twenty-three years but much closer in age than some of the other young women who had circulated around me, but more importantly, she was a respected musician. I welcomed her knowledge and enthusiasm for music and performance and the direction that someone like her offered me. Having a serious pianist next to me appeased any fears about the future.

In time, my personal life became more isolated, with fewer friends, and I rarely saw the rest of my family. I had a new life, and I could not risk losing my only source of inspiration and support. Doing so would have meant losing myself in loneliness all over again. Two years after Lina's death, I sold our home and remarried.

My persistent knee problems forced me to slow down and change the nature of my performances. But I had a new accompanist who booked joint recitals at Montreal's Place des Arts and for the CBC. We recorded CDs and videos together, were featured in various magazine articles, and my reviews were as glowing as ever.

I began to have confidence in myself again and felt no longer alone, to the point that I stopped talking to Lina.

Chapter 17
Dissonance

Louis, why did you stop confiding in me? I would have understood your need for comfort and connection with another companion. How could you have forgotten me so quickly?

I imagined my mother asking my father these questions from the ethereal world she now inhabited.

When music and singing are not in sync, when the music is not in tempo with the singing, or the other way around, the sounds created are painful to the ears, especially to those who, like my mother, had sought harmony for their whole life. I wondered if Mother could sense the same discordant notes I felt a year or so after the start of my father's new relationship, first as faint background noise, then the noise growing louder and clearer until it became a painful screech on the ears.

For me the dissonance became audible when I visited their new home and saw that not one of the photos of the Quilico family that Mother had so lovingly framed were anywhere to be seen. It was disconcerting to me to see the family's past erased. Where had our happy days in Rome gone? The family's concert at the Arena? Our singing for the Queen of England, the father and son performance at the Met, and my many other performances alongside my father?

How my mother's lingering presence and association with the Quilico name must have grated on his new wife, I thought, and I felt shattered.

Immersed in my career as always and my family life on shaky ground, I felt a sudden painful awareness that life as I had known it was coming apart. The glue that had held the pieces of our lives together was dissolving.

Signs that Father was becoming isolated, not only from his family but from his closest friends, surfaced after a few months of their marriage. My father became more and more estranged from me as well. I hardly saw him anymore.

Mother, could you see from above what was happening to the gregarious man you knew, loved and had sustained all of your life, as he turned distant and sullen towards his family?
Oh, the hell of total oblivion that you must suffer!

Chapter 18
A New Life

Gino and I still performed a few times together, but ours had become only a professional relationship. I didn't recognize my son anymore. He was always on the run. I resented that he did not fully acknowledge that I had made a new life for myself. I could not fathom having to rely on my children for the rest of my life. I sensed unspoken resentment whenever we were in the same room, but I felt I had to forge a new life for myself.

With my new marriage, both my life and my career bounced back for a while. I appeared at the Met in 1993 and 1994 for *Adriana Lecouvreur*, *Tosca*, and *I Pagliacci*; in *Falstaff* in New Orleans; *The Barber of Seville* in Palm Beach and Tel Aviv and then in 1994 played *Rigoletto* for the 510th time, in Ottawa. It would be my last time. The entire sold-out house rose to its feet after Act II. *Opera Canada* wrote, " Louis Quilico in his sixty-ninth year remains a vocal and dramatic marvel. His *Rigoletto* will be remembered for decades…"

My knee pains worsened, and I could not climb stairs. I had to sleep on a cot on the main floor of the house and use a wheelchair for long walks. We visited specialists who couldn't offer me much hope of regaining perfect mobility, even with an operation. I still tried to keep up with my wife and sang concerts with her. She even wrote a book about me, my voice techniques, and my career accomplishments. I had never been much of a reader, let alone a writer. I gave her complete control of the writing and she managed everything in my life.

My need to sing and perform was as strong as ever, and I could not resign myself to retiring. I still sang in various benefit concerts that were not physically taxing, and I gave them my all as if I were singing at the Met!

Meanwhile, after a number of angry confrontations, my son and I became strangers. I often thought of my father and the silence that kept us apart for so long. Though my father and I reconciled after I became famous, the anger toward him that had built up over the years never dissipated completely. I visited him when he became ill and was at his side when he died, but it felt more like an act of duty than love.

Bitterness and resentment cut the same painful wedge between Gino and me. I followed his career from the many magazine stories and heard the news of his personal life from Donna and David. At some point, we stopped speaking to each other.

In 2000, I sang for a benefit concert with an enthusiastic choir conductor, Vincenzo Guzzo. I was especially happy to receive the invitation because the concert was held in an Italian church in Saint Leonard, not far from where I had lived with my parents and siblings when a singing career was just a dream, out of the realm of possibility, and where later the community named a street after me. It also reminded me of my singing with the Saint Jacques choir, where I first experienced the joy of song. I left the church at peace, fully satisfied with my performance. Sadly, it would be my last.

A few weeks later, I entered hospital for a knee operation that I hoped would help me regain at least some my youthful gait. While lying in bed, though, I realized that I had no family next to me the way we had surrounded Lina while she was ill. I cried at the loss, especially at the fact that Gino and I were still at odds, and resolved that once out of the hospital, I'd reach out to him, offer him my musical scores, that I knew he wanted. I entered the operating room with some fear, then saw all the lights above me, and pretended I was walking onto a lit stage. The doctors came in, everything became silent and hazy, and I went to sleep, forever.

Louis on the occasion of his investment as a
Companion of the Order of Canada-1975

Quilicot bicycle store on St. Denis Street, Montreal

Louis Quilico (senior) and the Quilicot Bicycle Club

Louis on boat crossing to Rome, 1949

Louis-1950s

Review in *The New York Times*—Winner at the Met Auditions, 1955

CANADIANS ABROAD
Winner at the Met

At a Manhattan radio studio one afternoon last week, Montreal-born Louis Quilico, 30, heard news to thrill the heart of any singer: Baritone Quilico had just won a $2,000 cash prize from the Metropolitan Opera Association and an invitation for a season's study at the Metropolitan's Kathryn Long Opera School. Aquiver over the

Tommy Weber

BARITONE QUILICO
For a choirboy, a cattle boat.

news, Quilico hurried out of the rehearsal studio, took a long walk to calm his nerves, then returned to join the second- and third-place winners in the season's final broadcast of the *Metropolitan Opera Auditions of the Air* (ABC).

For Louis Quilico, the award was a big boost in a career he first aimed for as a choirboy in Montreal's St. Jacques Church. Six years ago he worked his way to Italy and a year's study at Rome's Conservatorio di Santa Cecilia.

Back at work in his father's Montreal bicycle shop, Louis Quilico soon got another boost in the form of a provincial scholarship to study in New York. There he hurried from classes to a night job as elevator operator at the Hotel Statler. Occasional radio and television engagements, along with roles in summer musicals, helped pay the bills for Baritone Quilico, his wife Lina—a Canadian musician who acts as his accompanist and coach—and their 3½-year-old daughter. For the last three years Quilico has worked between singing engagements as a tinsmith in Jamaica, L.I. Louis Quilico may be able to put aside his overalls and tin shears before long. Although the Metropolitan guarantees no contracts to winners of its auditions, the 1953 and 1954 winners (Baritone Robert McFerrin, Tenor Albert Da Costa) both joined the Met this season.

TIME, APRIL 11, 1955

Louis in *Don Carlos* at the Paris
Opera, 1963

Louis and Gino in *Rigoletto*
Toronto, 1979

Donna Quilico

Donna's children,
Natasha and David

Louis at the Met in *Il Trovatore*, 1977

Louis and Gino for the Father and Son historic performance
of *Manon* at the Met, 1987

Louis and Gino after a performance for Queen Elizabeth II for
the repatriation of the Canadian Constitution, 1982

ACT III

Gino: Don Giovanni Meets Jean Valjean

Chapter 19
The Man and the Artist

There was no singing at my father's funeral in Toronto—no singing for a man who had lived every day of his adult life either practising, rehearsing, or performing his opera roles. He ate opera for breakfast, lunch, and dinner, accompanied by live music, provided by my mother. I was too emotional to speak, too hurt by his sudden death and the fact I had had no chance to reconcile with him before he died.

I cried silently. *Dad, why did we stop speaking to each other? How did we let the petty complaints and misunderstandings poison our precious father/son relationship? You were my hero, my teacher, my favourite singer. I honoured you and I adored you.*

No one in the family even knew my father had entered the hospital and I questioned why a man in his condition, suffering from high blood pressure and a borderline diabetic would attempt an operation that had no guarantee of success. Who made him take the risk? I was bitter and angry.

At the too gloomy funeral mass, I heard someone, a member of his wife's family say, "I knew Quilico, the man." I wanted to scream out, " How little you knew my father if you only knew him as a man."

I insisted we have another mass in Montreal. It was a celebratory mass, held at Notre Dame Cathedral with all the music, singing, pomp and solemnity due to my father. Gaetan Laperriere sang "*Avant de quitter ces lieux"* from *Faust*. It was the aria that had won my Father his first real success and entrance at the Met and now would accompany him in his last journey. I found the courage to speak up, and I started my eulogy with the words, "I knew Quilico, the man and the artist. He was unique as a person as there was no differentiating between the man and the artist."

Oh Mother, I've listened to the story of your accomplishments with admiration and tears! Father, I heard and have finally understood your struggles and pain!

While they were both alive, I was simply too preoccupied with living my own life that I took their love for granted. They gave so generously to me, Donna and David, never expecting anything in return and never reminding us of what it took them to get there. Taken up by the constant demands of their art they expended little time and energy on the past. As for me, it is only now at a distance that I can reflect on our life lived as an opera—an Italian opera—at times buffa, at times romantic, sometimes melodramatic and tragic, at all times full of love and passion.

Mom and Dad, you gave me everything I value in life, and I am forever grateful. Dad, without your gift of voice and mom's constant and loving coaching, I would not have made it as an opera singer. My road to success has not been as arduous as it was for you.
Now, let me tell you my side of the story, my pain, my joys!

Chapter 20
Stage Childhood

I was born in Flushing Meadows, New York, but my parents moved to Montreal before I could register even the faintest of images of our American life. I heard we lived in a large home in the style of a *Father Knows Best* suburb. Though unrecalled in my memory, that place of birth secured me dual American and Canadian citizenship as well as passports from both countries. Of my childhood time in Montreal, I remember the many bicycles and pedal cars in my grandfather's store, the model trains with which my father and I played, and the constant movement of people and wheels. I have vague images of the *ruelles* in the back of the store with the messy piles of old tires and the garbage trucks that passed by, but I remember vividly that I wanted to be a garbage man, so I could jump on and off a huge truck. Then my father opened his bicycle store. There were fewer bicycles for sale than at grandfather's store and fewer people coming by, but lots of space for my sister and me to race around on our tricycles.

"It's my store," my father often said, "with nobody to boss me around." But then I remember the discussions between my parents about closing the store to move again, always moving away to somewhere new. Where this time? It turns out it was the United Kingdom.

Memories of London as a child are as foggy as its weather. There are hazy images of double-decker buses, billboards, neon lights, and traffic of

Piccadilly Circus, and the ever-present fog, which I thought was normal and caused by the smoke from chimneys. Having a good ear for sounds, even in the short time we lived there, I managed to pick up a British accent. But when I think of Paris, the family's next move, the city comes into focus clear and bright, especially my first visit to an opera house: the humongous chandelier, the painted ceilings, the sculptured wall sconces. I had never seen such a splendid palace before, a palace fit for a king.

"Your Father lives here…for a while. It's where he works," my mother told me.

This was news to me. I knew some parents who worked as doctors, plumbers, electricians. I always thought my parents worked at home, my mother playing the piano, and my father singing in the living room. It's what they did every day. Music was their job, a natural part of our lives. I never questioned where they performed. But to work in a palace as magnificent as the opera house, I was in awe! There we sat on plush seats with shimmering lights all around us and people dressed in beautiful clothes, waiting expectantly for something to happen. When the big curtains opened, and I saw Dad in full costume as the Marquis de Posa, I followed his every move in a daze. When he was killed, I crouched in my seat in fear and looked up to my mother, but she didn't seem worried. She patted my hand as if to say, "It's okay." After the loud applause when he came out bowing at the end, I felt that what he did was really special; my dad was special, and I was part of this opulent universe! It made me feel special, too.

"Wow!" I said over and over again to myself while my mother smiled.

As children, we had moved from country to country, making new friends then leaving them behind, without understanding the magnitude and grandeur of our parents' project until that moment.

Life in Paris was not kind to me. I looked too American for the other kids and even for my teacher. Was it my running shoes, my baseball cap, my haircut? I don't know. My first language had been French, but I soon realized that I spoke differently than the Parisian kids. They must have wondered what I was all about, an American kid who spoke with a British accent and French with an even funnier pronunciation. I didn't know what to think myself. Was I Canadian, French Canadian, British, American, Italian? I had a bit of all those identities but wasn't able to fully embrace any of them.

My sister and I were inseparable. We were each other's best friends though we played tricks on each other. In London and Paris, in our small living quarters, we spent a lot of our time in the evenings doing arts and crafts together. My drawings never measured up to hers, and I was jealous of her natural talent. She also liked writing little poems. On one of our travels, Mom and Dad brought us to Venice. Like most tourists, we rode a gondola. We watched with glee as a huge rat swam by us in the water. Back in the hotel, Donna wrote a poem about a rat that made us all howl with laughter. Donna was also a very talented ballerina. She studied in Montreal with Madame Ludmilla Chiriaef of Les Grands Ballets Canadiens, and she continued lessons in London and Paris. In London, I even took ballet lessons with her. I looked up at my older sister and felt she had so much talent, and I had none. She was my idol!

Soon after Paris, we moved to Italy. Learning to speak Italian would be yet another thing to adapt to, but my parents had smartened up by then and sent us to American schools, Notre Dame for me, run by priests, and Marymount for my sister. After that, life was just dandy! I was one of the most popular guys around the school and in my neighbourhood, especially after I inherited a Solex scooter from my sister. She moved on to a Vespa. Maybe living in various cities had given me resilience and an ability to make new friends quickly and effortlessly. Maybe knowing it might just be short term, impermanent, added a layer of safety. Was that the key? Were we spoiled as kids? We most surely were. Were the gifts compensation for the many moves and our parents' absences? Possibly, but I had a ball in Rome.

It was the time when Rome was known as the "Hollywood in the Tiber," as in the movie *Roman Holiday* with Audrey Hepburn and Gregory Peck riding on a Vespa around the city. Movie screens all around the world projected the seven hills and wonders of Rome. Restaurants and cafés along Via Veneto teemed with paparazzi, at the ready to photograph the latest American starlet. *La Dolce Vita* was not just a movie, but the life many Italians aspired to live after their country had been ravished by war and starvation. In the heady rush toward an economic boom, Italians hungered for the good things of life, and we were in a city that was living life to the fullest.

We lived in the EUR sector of Rome, a modernist district of the city where we had the best of two worlds—an apartment in a new neighbourhood in one of the most ancient cities in Europe. For once, I felt we were part of a community. I loved getting in the car with the family on weekends and driving to the beach in Ostia, where we had a boat moored in a small marina. We sang loudly in the car while other cars honked, waved, and smiled at father's booming "*O sole mio!*"

I had my first girlfriend in Rome. Is there anything more romantic than to kiss a girl by sunset in Rome? At eleven years of age, I was on my way to becoming a Latin lover in an Italian movie. Becoming a movie star was not just a fantasy but a real possibility in Rome, I thought. Cinecittà, where movies were made, was just a suburb away from the city. One afternoon, without permission from my parents, I set out on my Solex to go there. I had heard from my friends that they were auditioning for extras on a movie set for a spaghetti western. Unfortunately, my sense of direction was not up to par, and I never found the movie set nor Cinecittà. That didn't stop me from dreaming of a future acting career. Then all of a sudden, my movie-star life is interrupted by these words.

"I think I'm pregnant," Donna announces to my parents.

It was like a director yelling, "Cut!" At first I thought it was a joke. Then seeing my parents' worried faces, I too felt their frustration and bitter disappointment.

How did it happen? I also worried. By a kiss? Could my girlfriend be pregnant, too?

After a quick trip to Las Vegas where we only saw the glittering casinos from the streets, my fifteen-year-old sister is now married. That should have solved everything, but no.... All of a sudden, I have to leave my Solex behind, give it to my friend, Marco. My sister has changed over one summer, and it seems that all our lives suddenly change too. There are no more drives to the beach in Ostia in a convertible singing *O Sole Mio* with Dad, no more evenings eating gelato late at night after eating platefuls of pasta *carbonara*. Worst of all? No more sunset kisses in Piazza di Spagna.

The family packs up again, and I find myself on a plane with a sour-faced family. My only consolation: my mother buys me a dozen packages of Dentyne chewing gum as soon as we land in New York.

Chapter 21
A New, Crazy World

I was all of twelve years old, an innocent, naïve kid who spoke English with a strong Italian accent. The Big Apple had lots to promise a nearly teenage boy: fancy cars, television, blue jeans—hard to get in Italy—and lots of junk food.

But adjustment in school didn't come easily for me. I found myself an outsider again with classmates a year younger than me as I was held back by one year. Just like in France, I was bullied because of my accent and speech patterns. Some kids even made fun of my name, Gino, too Italian and girly, like Gina Lollobrigida. I felt myself a misfit in many other ways and yearned for my Italian life. I had learned to listen to classical music, behave in a polite, gentlemanly manner towards elders, and open doors for girls and women. My new friends thought only of playing baseball and smoking pot. I had never received any type of sex education, apart from the alarming "I am pregnant" from my more sexually aware older sister. Losing one's virginity was still considered a dishonour in Italy, while in New York, it was something to boast about. I was the only nerdy oddball male virgin in my new circle of friends. Maybe it was all big talk on their part, but I felt inferior.

In short, I was a skinny kid with European manners, thrown into inner-city New York by parents preoccupied with a teenage mother for a daughter and raising their grandchild as their own, all the while still pursuing a musical career in competitive New York City. The magic of Paris, the exuberance of Rome, had morphed into the dizzying and sleazy neon lights of Times Square with its drug pushers, prostitutes, and blatant "buy me, buy me" culture. Perhaps I bought into that culture too quickly, but what could you expect? I was just a kid who wanted nothing more than to fit in.

Maybe playing guitar in a rock band would gain me admission to this new, crazy world. School didn't carry much luster, and I skipped as many days as I could without getting caught. I no longer wanted to be called Gino: such a lame name for a rock star. What could be more American than John, my baptismal first name of Giovanni. I became John to my new friends, and I wore only blue jeans and chewed lots of bubble gum.

Did I want to distance myself from the other two Luigi's, my grandfather and father, or simply sound more American? Whatever the reason, John stayed with me right up to my university days. Still, to look cool and be part of the gang, I took to drinking whiskey and experimenting with sex.

Not surprisingly, I fell behind in school. An IQ test indicated the intellect of a 6-year-old, but how could I be expected to perform well on a test skewed to Americans? The questions were based on the American curriculum, which I knew little about. I had attended an American school in Italy for such a brief period, and I had never fully mastered the English language.

Sorry, Mom, Dad, if I disappointed you, but there had been too many disruptions in my life, too many false starts and sudden departures.

My mother hired a tutor to help me succeed in American history and geography but with little result as I was still in a confused haze. I had been taught British, French, and Italian history, which spanned centuries with larger-than-life characters—kings, queens, Napoleon, Garibaldi—some of whom had made it into the movies, but did Americans really call cowboy movies history?

Then one day, my mother received a call from the principal's office summoning all of us, her, my father, and me, to a meeting. "It's urgent that the three of you attend," the secretary told her. I saw the bewilderment in my mother's eyes and then the look of frustration on her face when she learned that I had skipped school for almost a year.

My father looked more hurt than angry. He had always been a good loving father, but he was also so absorbed in his career and often oblivious of my daily activities. Was it guilt at the turn my life was taking? Was it guilt because my mother had been too preoccupied with his career to notice the changes in me and Donna that made her turn to Dad as we left the office and say, "What is happening to this family?"

There is another scene of my movie I wish I could cut out.

A few months later, on a holiday in Florida when I had just turned fourteen, Donna and I argued and she turned around and told Mom I was using drugs and even experimenting with LSD. My mother searched my suitcase and found a joint and some pills. I confessed that part of my New York street education had involved drugs, and I did my share of smoking pot and even taking cocaine, uppers and downers, but I reassured her, "I stopped short of using needles."

"Well, I'm thankful for that! No wonder you had such little interest in scholastic life!" She threw her hands up.

I could tell this discovery crushed my mother, and she could no longer contain her anger. She gave me a piece of her mind in her direct and no-nonsense manner: "You better shape up, or I'll leave you in the streets begging for money!" I saw firmness in her eyes. I knew she meant business, and I resolved to clean up my act, or at least try to.

As devastated as they were by the discovery of my dabbling with drugs, both my parents handled the situation with love. "I know you have a very active and creative imagination and have to try things out for yourself, but use that creativity to find your niche in life," Mom said to me.

It's what I wanted more than anything else, except that I hadn't yet identified any niche into which I could fit.

When I turned fifteen, my father and mother accepted prestigious teaching positions at the University of Toronto, and we were off again! The family moved to Toronto. I now had to tackle Canadian history and geography! The British North American Act, the Statute of Westminster, the building of the Canadian Pacific Railway—all topics that bored me to death. Even less than American history, none of these events had been momentous enough for a TV series, let alone a Hollywood movie. Louis Riel sounded interesting, but I never really understood his story. Was he French, Native, Canadian? Why did they hang him? It all sounded too complicated for me, and, quite honestly, I didn't give a crap. I had difficulty with another educational transition, but never had problems finding friends that helped me perpetuate the pattern I had adopted in New York and then some!

At sixteen, I had had enough of school. I didn't like asking my parents for money, so it was an easy decision to quit school to look for work. Neither parent tried to stop me. They understood I had to find my own way. I began a long succession of temporary jobs to earn my own spending money. No job was too menial. I started pumping gas at an Esso Garage. The owner of the garage, Ed Lewiki, took a liking to me and promised he'd promote me to assistant mechanic and home service. Meanwhile, as training, he had me cleaning chimneys, putting up storm windows, washing windows, shoveling snow.

Yes, I was earning my own spending money, but I can't say that I felt good about myself and the life I was leading. I realized that, somehow, I had to upgrade my education and eventually went to Seneca College to obtain my high school diploma. A mellow hippie of a teacher conducted a very relaxed class. He may not have had much to offer in academic brilliance, but he loved the Beatles. He even allowed us to smoke cigarettes in class, a bad habit I had developed by then and only quit at 19. Oh well, the times they were "a-changing." Like thousands of other young people at the time, I was searching for answers to the existential questions that were "blowing in the wind." Slowly, my ears became more and more attuned to the inevitable call of music. It was in my bones and in my blood, waiting to be heard.

I started playing Beatles tunes on my guitar and formed a band with friends. We played rock music at dances—Deep Purple, Uriah Heep, Black Sabbath–and I hammered on through Zeppelin's famous "Stairway to Heaven." We even wrote our own songs, but we didn't achieve the fame I hoped for. My friends were lame ducks without any real passion or the discipline to make it in the music industry. I soon became fed up with that amateur scene.

After a couple of years, when no interesting jobs came my way, Dad convinced me to try singing opera and start from the bottom by auditioning for the Canadian Opera Company's extra chorus. The money was good—$2,000 for singing in two operas for about one month— excellent money for me. My voice was still not fully developed, but the chorus needed singers with stage presence who sang on pitch, loudly and not necessarily well, which described my singing ability at the time. I learned the aria "*Non piu andrai*" from *The Marriage of Figaro*.

What a surprise and relief when I auditioned for the conductor Ernesto Barbini, and for the Canadian Opera director Herman Geiger-Torel, and they accepted me! They might have been curious about Louis Quilico's son wanting to sing, because it was not typical for a general director to sit in on and for extra chorus. At the time, I still sang in my pop music voice and had no formal musical training, though I had studied a bit of piano as a child.

When I first went on stage in *Fidelio* and *Gotterdammerung* and saw 3,000 people in the audience, I caught the performance bug. The idea of singing opera was slowly seducing me, and I even asked my father to teach me. One day I taped my voice. I sang the only aria I knew well and which I had also sang for my audition, "*Non piu adrai*," but I wanted to hide under the kitchen table when I played it back. I was so embarrassed by the voice I heard. I thought, "Who is this guy with the funny voice?" I couldn't connect his voice to me or to the image of me I had wanted to project up to then. I was ashamed of my voice and turned the recorder off before the end of the song. The whole idea of wanting to be an opera singer was ridiculous! I took off to Montreal to get away from it all and try my luck there.

Chapter 22
Anne-Marie

The year spent in Montreal turned out to be an eventful one for my romantic life. I fell hopelessly in love with a ballerina. Language problems still plagued me. While in New York, my private tutors had encouraged me to forsake my French and Italian languages to master English better. I realized this was something of a mistake in Montreal, where it was hard to get by without French. I took a job as a debonair Tip Top tailors salesman. They gave me a suit to wear, and I looked the part, though my heart was not in it, and I quit after a few months. It was, however, good practice for my French.

I envied my sister, who had been accepted to study ballet at the Les Grands Ballets Canadiens in Montreal, though she didn't seem to be particularly happy there. She missed her baby, David, who was being raised by our parents. I wanted to enter her artistic world, and she introduced me to her friend, Anne-Marie, who was also studying ballet but with the Compagnie de Danse Eddy Toussaint. My parents were skeptical when I first introduced her to them. She was six years older than me, and she very quickly displayed a moody and querulous personality. If I said, "What a sunny day," she'd answer, "It's shitty." And we argued continuously from the very start. At the time, she was a beautiful woman and a dancer and I was delivering dentures for a dental company. There were no more job opportunities in Montreal, and I was in awe of her, so I convinced her to move to Toronto with me.

Without jobs or even job prospects in Toronto, we lived with my parents for three years. Despite the constant fighting with Anne-Marie, I made some crucial changes in my life while we were together. Cutting my long hair was a first step, followed by cutting ties with my old friends, which led to cutting out drugs for good. In that regard, she had a healthy influence on me.

Another benefit of my relationship with Anne-Marie is that she slowly encouraged me to sing again. For that, I will be forever grateful. She convinced me that my singing voice was not as ridiculous as it had sounded on those tapes. I was somewhat shy about going to my father again after I had made such a scene, so, as always, I went to Mother first. She encouraged me to ask my father for his help.

Thank you, Dad, for listening to me again and not laughing at my voice as I had feared.

For two years, my father gave me private lessons at home focusing on only technique. This was my true apprenticeship. For six months we worked on breathing and for six months on opening the throat so that I was able to produce my first operatic sounds. My mother took over to teach me repertoire. Only when she felt I was ready did she advise me to apply for the Toronto's Faculty of Music Opera Department.

My next audition was for Connie Fisher and James Craig who headed the opera department. Before making a final decision, James Craig asked me to come back after learning the scene from the musically difficult opera *Albert Herring* by Benjamin Britten where Sid, my character, makes an entrance. He had this opera in mind for me in my first year and it's an important scene. He figured I might need a long time to learn it. However, I surprised him when after three days, I sang the whole scene from memory. Professor Craig was impressed, and I was accepted into the program and got the part. I had the best voice coach and best musical coach possible, my mother and my father.

By the second year, I was ready to sing the title role of Don Giovanni—my first encounter with this role. I was 23 years old, the same age as the first Giovanni created by Mozart.

From the beginning, I took my singing and my characters very seriously and studied very intensely. To inspire me I went to see my friend Frank Augustyn who was premier dancer at the Toronto National Ballet with the ballerina Karen Kain. Frank was dancing the title role in the ballet *Don Juan*. To this day, I think about the presence a dancer has on stage. It's all about posture!

I don't know how many opera lovers fully understand the discipline and work involved in preparing to sing a full opera on stage—it is so different from simply singing an aria. When I prepare a role for the first time, the first task is to get the notes and the rhythm right. I would do this with my mother or another pianist when she was not available. Then, I'd memorize the notes, after which time I would start putting the words to the notes. It's a long and tedious process to memorize it all, the music and the words. Once you master this part, you must focus on putting it all together in your voice, that is, in the breathing. The breath is the most important preparation of musical expression. It is very technical but extremely necessary to be precise in your breathing. The fun part comes when emotion is added through the notes, the words and the breath, all while remembering the vocal techniques.

I learned many stage tricks in those early days from Connie Fisher and Michael Albano: especially how to angle and tilt my body for full effect, fall on my knees when singing the Valentin aria in *Faust*, sing to a person beside you without looking at that person to best direct the voice—all valuable lessons that have helped me throughout my career. Being part of a family devoted to the art of opera served me well. It made me fully understand the training required and gave me an appreciation of the "business" of opera and all that it entails.

At the beginning, I sensed some jealousy amongst the other students because of my father's connections, but there was no doubt that I was the best-prepared singer. I had become very serious about my new chosen path and worked very diligently on my voice training. At last, I felt in my element, I had found my niche. I worked on staging and characterization with Connie Fisher and Michael Albano, and music with pianist coach and conductor Jim Craig.

Dad, more than anything else, I never wanted to ride on your coattails.

My dad was always on hand with invaluable suggestions and tricks of the trade that only an experienced artist could impart. I remember the dress rehearsal for my performance of Don Giovanni. He told me to stand still in the middle of the stage during the champagne aria, with the champagne glass in hand, instead of moving around as the stage director wanted. I followed his advice. This was my first experience of acting like a Divo with a director! My father taught me well. The director never quite forgave me for overriding his staging, but not only did I experience the thrill of my first tremendous success as Don Giovanni, but I walked around like a Don for days after. I was hooked on opera!

I flourished in the musical atmosphere of the university. But oh, the personality clashes and arguments between Anne-Marie and me! She was jealous of my friends and rising success and made me distance myself from all of them. She had this uncanny habit of getting into an argument just before a serious audition. Ours became a toxic relationship.

In June 1977, I auditioned for Maureen Forrester—my first professional paid engagement as a soloist. I debuted as Mr. Gabineau in a production of *The Medium* by the Comus Music Theatre, produced by the MacMillan Theatre and later by CBC Television. My father reminded me that Maureen Forrester had also given him his first concert debut, and I felt proud and honored to sing next to her. My star was rising slowly but surely, though I was still not earning enough to support myself and Anne-Marie. I didn't let this discourage me. I was lucky to be able to count on my parents.

After three years of living with Anne-Marie, I was still determined to marry her despite our frequent screaming matches. Though not fully convinced that we'd make a good married couple, in 1978, my parents offered us a dream wedding with some of the most important opera personalities in attendance. My parents also generously gave us the down payment for our own condo. They did all they could to help make the marriage work.

Thanks to some significant roles, my career began to take off, and I was becoming in demand as a singer. That same year, the Cincinnati Opera accepted me for their Young American Artists Program (YAAP), and Anne-Marie accompanied me. I studied classic dancing for the stage like the waltz and period dancing like the *minuetto*, mime, and even Broadway-style choreographies.

My bohemian life as an artist travelling away from home had begun. Meanwhile, my talented young wife struggled with an artistic career that as yet lacked traction. Was there resentment at my success while her career was lagging?

All I know is that Cincinnati would become my Waterloo.

Jealousy, love, and betrayal are some of the most recurring themes in opera, so are brash and macho male roles, like Escamillo, Figaro, and

Don Giovanni. In Cincinnati, I was finally interpreting characters and their roles helped me master my insecurities. However, the fights with Anne-Marie intensified, her behaviour becoming more erratic, even suspicious.

"I'm going out for a walk," she told me one afternoon. "Have to get some aspirin."

"I'll come with you."

"No, I need time to be on my own."

The weather was not very pleasant, and it was not in her habit to go walking at that time of day.

I followed her from a window. She turned the corner. I leaned out the window and could just catch a glimpse of her walking briskly past the corner drug store. She did not go in. There was a telephone booth a few metres away. I could only see part of it, but it looked as if she stopped there and disappeared into the booth. Within a few minutes, she came back in view and returned home. She never stopped by the pharmacy for her aspirin. I found a full bottle in her cosmetic bag

I could not question her without disclosing that I spied on her, which would have started a vicious fight, so I let it be. A week later, she had a dentist appointment and would be out all afternoon. It just so happened to be on a rare afternoon when I was not rehearsing. I decided to go to the theatre rather than stay home by myself. I knew that the rest of the cast was rehearsing. I thought I'd catch them on their break and have lunch with them. From a distance and to my surprise, I saw Anne-Marie waiting outside the theatre. I stayed back and watched. Within a few minutes, who comes out to join her, but one of my friends from the company: a man who sang bass and will remain nameless, tall, skinny, and nerdy. I had nicknamed him the twerp when he tried hard to ingratiate himself with me. He joined her. They kissed and walked away. Should I follow them? Confront them? I didn't know what to do. It can't be, I told myself. This guy can't possibly be cuckolding me! I was the Don Giovanni par excellence, for crying out loud! All the girls swooned over me while he was only a third-rate bass singing a secondary role. What did she see in him that I didn't have? Furthermore, I had been faithful to her, even if I thought of myself as a Don Giovanni.

There must be an explanation, I thought. Maybe the twerp was helping her in one of her dancing roles. Perhaps they were only friends, and she was confiding in him about our constant fighting, about things she was too intimidated to discuss with me, to get the opinion of another man whom she thought was a friend of mine. High hopes, I thought. But I confided in women friends at times, so why could she not confide in a man friend? Should I catch up to them, I wondered, and just pretend I was passing them by without making a fuss, or just stay back? But what was that kiss about?

The temptation to follow them was too strong. I kept a distance without losing sight of them. They held hands as they walked and often stopped to kiss each other on the lips, my anxiety rising with each step I took, with each kiss I saw. Would I wake up from this? They seemed to be walking around in a circle; then, they stopped at the dingy boarding house where I knew he lived, just a street away from our apartment. I knew other members of the chorus who rented there. I had often joined them in their rooms at the end of rehearsal for drinks. The love birds entered the building happy and smiling, she giggling. I hadn't seen her smile like this in ages. There could be no doubt that they were having an affair. Still, I asked myself: Why with him? I waited outside for a few minutes to compose myself before knocking at the door.. I'd pretend I was just passing by and stopped to say hello to the twerp.

What followed was worthy of any *opera buffa*.

He answered the door, a look of surprise on his face, or was it fear? I walked right in without being invited and saw Anne-Marie sitting on his bed. She suddenly stood up as if caught raiding the cookie jar.

The twerp ran to her, put his arms around her as if to protect her from my anger.

I forgot to pretend I was there by chance.

"Is this where you get your teeth checked," I asked, "your cavities filled?"

"We're in love," he butted in quickly as if to protect her.

"In love? You mean you're not just having a good time in the sack behind my back?"

"No, it's not what you think. We're truly, truly in love."

I would have taken the admission of a good time in the sack much easier than them being truly, truly in love.

This is where my Latin lover and Italian blood came to a boil! I thrust myself at him and shocked him with a jab under his jaw, a move I had learned in a boxing class at Notre Dame. I had boxed there until my mother took me out of the team for the Golden Glove because of severe nosebleeds. I knocked him off balance, and he fell on the bed on top of Anne-Marie, who shrieked. He jumped up quickly and clearly wanted to counter-attack. He positioned himself as if for a duel. I did the same. We had both studied fencing and rehearsed duel positions many times, but ours became more of a dance than a fight without the fake swords. I lost patience and jabbed him again on the chin. Hearing Anne-Marie's screams, some choir members ran into the room and tried to separate us. But I was too enraged and kicked and punched everyone in sight. One guy managed to take the twerp away and into the corridor.

I followed them and yelled, "Fight me if you can, you coward."

Meanwhile, other residents came out of their rooms, watching the commotion. Some yelled at us to stop; others cheered us to go on. I couldn't stop fighting. I wanted to see him on the floor, holding him down with my foot so that I could spit on his face, but it was me that three guys threw down and pinned on the floor. All I could do was scream out at the top of my voice, "You can have her. You deserve each other!"

Chapter 23
Carmen

The honour-saving duel had been exhilarating, but it was the twerp who walked out with the damsel while I was left on the floor with only cautious expressions of commiseration from my friends. There could be neither a possibility nor a desire for a rematch. Along with the battle, I lost the war, the woman, and my dignity.

I couldn't face anyone I knew, and I wanted to disappear. I told one of my colleagues to advise the director not to look for me. Back in my hotel, I dreaded having to confront my wife again when she'd come back to get her things. Neither could I bear the thought of returning to the opera theatre and being humiliated by the two-faced people inside it. I quickly packed a bag and set out on a seven-hour drive to Toronto at a ridiculous and dangerous high speed, pushing fate, almost wanting to crash. Once I arrived, I didn't have the nerve to show up at my parent's place in my sad condition and at that hour of the night. I checked into a second-class hotel. Having had nothing to eat since the morning, I looked for a restaurant but stopped at a nearby bar instead. They kicked me out after only an hour. I had forgotten how early bars closed at night in super-boring Toronto. A friendly bartender named Ruby helped me out and walked me to my hotel. My room had a pungent stench I couldn't identify. Maybe it's me, I thought and took a quick shower to wash Cincinnati off my body. The odour in the room persisted, embedded in the dingy and worn-out carpet. I felt like the jilted second-class baritone that I was, cuckolded by a third-class base who usurped my role as husband and, most importantly, as lover. Sleep saved me from crying all night long, and I only woke up in the late afternoon the next day. I resolved to return to the bar to drink and find some beautiful woman to sleep with. There were many gorgeous girls available but strangely, I felt no desire for them. All I really wanted was to be left alone while signalling Ruby to pour me more drinks.

I sunk into a deep dark hole, threatened by some invisible force that I couldn't explain. It wasn't just the loss of my wife's love that caused me gloom and misery, but a deep, paralyzing fear that I had lost myself, and that perhaps I'd never sing again. Then the terror took on the shape of a strange being floating around me, sucking the life out of me to feed itself, like a vampire that can only survive on another's blood. I first saw his shadow in my dream, or what I thought to be a shadow and what I thought to be a dream. When I woke up trembling, I still felt the same dark presence in the room: a slim, tall, overpowering shadow. I turned on all the lights, and beneath the large grey patches of peeling paint, I saw shadows etched on the dirty walls. In time, the lingering odour in the room reminded me of moldy potatoes. Maybe it's the smell of decaying ghosts trying to hold on to life, I thought. I had never believed in ghosts before. I fell back to sleep at dawn and slept all day. At dusk, I left the room and walked back to the bar, looking behind me, sure I was being stalked by the dark menacing shadow. I stayed at the bar until closing time, surviving on peanuts and brandy. I then crouched in bed as if in a hole in the ground, but only the booze could make me feel safe, even as I was aware of drowning in it. I repeated this routine. Was it two, three nights? I lost track of time. I don't remember. Panic set in and sucked all the energy out of me. How could I ever sing again, make love again? Luckily my parents thought I was in Cincinnati and were still unaware of what was happening. How disappointed would they be with me for having a failed marriage after not eve a year, a marriage they had discouraged from the start, and how infuriated that I had walked out on my first important singing opportunity? I had messed up on both counts.

The only person that showed any interest in me was Ruby, the bartender, a slender red-haired woman with heavy voluptuous breasts that seemed to tip her forward as she walked me to my hotel at night. She spoke in a warm voice and seemed to be sincerely worried about me.

One evening, the last one I'd spend at the bar, she asked me softly, "Why are you crying in your Armagnac? Have you lost someone or something?"

"Yes, I've lost my ego."

"Is it that important?"

"For me, it's everything. I can't sing without it, and I can't ever make love again. Some worthless twerp stole it, and I'm afraid I'll never get it back."

"I can't do anything about the singing, but I can take you to your hotel and keep you company for a while."

"My hotel gives me the creeps. It's no place to bring a lady."

"I'll take you to my place, then."

I put myself in her loving and expert arms. There was no sex that first night. Hers was truly the kind gesture of a woman who wanted to help me. We did make love the next evening and the day after. I told her my whole story while crying in her arms, and I lost myself in the curves of her generous breasts. I let her caress me gently and make love to me without counting the days or nights. She fed me food and passion without any demands. With her every touch, bit by bit, the stress of my rising career, the frustrations at Anne-Marie's flare-ups, the pent-up anger and hate for her betrayal dissipated. Most importantly, I stopped dreaming of the threatening tall shadow. By listening to my body and making love to me, she truly saved my soul and spirit and gave me strength. After a week or so of pure sex, I felt ready to face my world again, leave the scary dark cavern in which I had fallen and maybe sing again.

I never gave her my full name and neither did she ask, but on the last day, I asked her, "Is Ruby your real name?"

"No," she laughed, "that's my bar name. I'm Carmen."

"And I'm Escamillo," I replied and bellowed out the Toreador song.

Toreador, on guard! Toreador, Toreador!
And dream well, yes, dream of fighting
There is a pair of black eyes watching you,
That await your love.
Toreador, love awaits you!

Chapter 24
My Big Break

Carmen, her real name, and my sex drive had managed to heal my wounded ego and cure me of my fears. I never thanked her enough. I called my parents, and without revealing all the details of those last days, I told them that I couldn't live with Anne-Marie anymore. My mother didn't ask any questions as if she had expected this outcome but advised me to make a clean break.

"Her energy has been toxic for you. Surround yourself with positive forces from now on."

My parents didn't try to change my mind when I told them I decided to cancel my contract with the Cincinnati Young American Artists Program. I left Anne-Marie there with the twerp with some feelings of anguish and shame at having to divorce her in the same year that we had officially married. I followed my mother's guidance and let her have everything we had accumulated together and even got rid of the clothes I had worn when we were together. Soon after filing divorce papers, I went to a clothing store and bought an entirely new wardrobe.

When I felt comfortable talking to my mother about the semi-paranormal experience that had paralyzed me at the hotel, she didn't make light of it. "Harvest the positive vibrations within you to overcome the negative energies that life is bound to throw your way on occasion. Your father faced his fears head-on and found his energy when he bounced his voice back against the wall in Flushing Meadows. Trust yourself and your talent. No one can take it away from you because it's part of you, part of your body. Make it part of your mind. Above all, fight the dark with the light."

Leaving Cincinnati was not the most favourable decision for my young career. I knew that my parents were aware that it could derail the progress we had made together. Yet Cincinnati had become an emblem of a poisonous relationship whose head needed to be severed to safeguard my mental welfare.

I'm forever grateful for your understanding, Mom, Dad.

Their love sustained me and warded off the bouts of depression—at least for a while. They gave me the strength and resolution to start anew in the face of pain and disappointment. I knew that without resilience, many careers had faltered, while mine was still growing, albeit small step by small step. From then on, I saw my mother as my guardian angel, my angel of light! My star had started its ascent, not shooting instantly to disappear just as quickly out of sight, but rising organically and more brilliant with each new phase.

Soon after my return from Cincinnati, Joel Bloch of Shaw Concerts offered me a debut in Milwaukee singing Papageno in *The Magic Flute*. Starring as the Queen of the Night was June Anderson. I toured eastern Canada and the United States as the Count in *The Marriage of Figaro*, a production by the Canadian Opera Company. Then in the fall of 1979, the COC offered me Escamillo in *Carmen* at the Royal Alexandra Theatre with mezzo-soprano Judith Forster. I revelled in the role, and most importantly, I was having fun!

Many of the singers in the chorus and those who sang smaller, but essential parts, were fellow students, and I had a wonderful time singing alongside them. On the last night of the performance, Frasquitta and Mercedes, two of Carmen's gypsy girlfriends, decided to play a prank on me. When I came to sing the Toreador's famous aria, they both exposed strange fake tattoos on their breasts, meant to make me laugh as I held them in my arms, singing my heart out. Meanwhile, the best part of the joke was happening unseen! They snuck their hands behind me and up between my legs to squeeze my most sensitive and private parts as I sang the high notes. And yes, my voice went higher with each squeeze.

The most important take-away from the prank was that I was enjoying singing and living again!

My big international break came when my friend Jean Verreau and I auditioned for Bernard Lefort of the Paris Opera. After singing two lines of "The Drinking Song" from Thomas' *Hamlet*, Lefort offered me a three-year contract with the Paris Opera. I couldn't believe my good fortune; it was the breakthrough I had dreamed of!

I lost no time packing my bags for Paris. I still had to audition for the first part they had in mind for me, in the contemporary opera *L'Héritière* by Michel Damase. I took a taxi from Orly airport, and before going to my hotel, I had the taxi driver pass by the Paris Opera to admire the opulent building. I couldn't contain my excitement. This would be my special Opera House just as the Met became special for my father. It was here that as a child, I had first felt enthralled by the lights, costumes, and magic of opera and had felt a sense of pride in my father's singing.

The audition turned out to be quite an unexpected adventure, and my entrance not as grand as I had imagined.

I was very anxious on the morning of the audition. I had vomited all night and slept barely two hours, not because of drinking or stress, but because I had eaten some bad mussels. I had been dreadfully sick from both ends of my body, and my stomach still felt unsettled in the morning.

Bernard Lefort thought I would be right for a high baritone role. I was young and could sing the high notes, with or without the help of my two gypsy friends. Dressed formally in my suit and tie, I arrived at the Opera Comique, ready for the audition. The Opera Comique was an old theatre where Georges Bizet had created *Carmen* and many other great operas, but it was an aged building with no modern amenities, as I soon found out. A little nervous about the audition, I decided to go to the bathroom to freshen up. On my way up the stairs, I spotted the toilet door and entered. To my surprise, it had no toilet bowl. The bathroom consisted of a hole in the middle of the floor with two islands on each side to stand on. I had never seen this type of toilet before, and it took me a few seconds to figure out how to position myself. Quite primitive, I thought. Luckily, I only had to pee. I put my feet on the islands and peed in the hole while standing, proud of myself for having aimed so well... until I flushed. I had remained with my feet solidly placed on the two islands while I pulled the chain.

"Oh, crap!" I yelled. The jet of water sprayed so hard that it drenched my shoes and pants! "What do I do now?" I thought. It was too late to go back home and change. Squish, squash, my shoes squeaked as I proceeded to the audition on the top floor. I entered the room. Everybody was there, the director of the opera house, the maestro, the casting director. Still, like a Divo, I made a grand entrance in my wet pants and shoes. Everybody in the room burst into laughter at another foolish American who didn't know about the primitive precursor of the famous French pissoirs.

Surprisingly, despite the embarrassing entrance, I sang incredibly well, maybe because my all-night vomiting helped open up my throat. I have often used the story as a joke in my singing classes. I tell students that to have a crystal-clear voice, it helps to be retching all night first.

In the end, I got the part.

When I recounted the story to my father, he reminded me that he too won an audition with drenched pant legs, in his case it was the Met and the rain. Emboldened by the opportunities opening up for me in Paris, I returned to Toronto to collect my things and to attend to some prior commitments. Outwardly, I was cocky, sure of myself, and felt incredibly handsome in my new wardrobe! Deep inside me, the prospect of being alone in Paris scared me. I feared sinking into the lonely hole of insecurity. I was not born to live alone. I craved companionship, conversation, affection, and real love.

The opportunity presented itself as if I had ordered it.

Chapter 25
Kathryn

Donning white shoes, white pants, and a white shirt, I attended a Canadian Opera Company event held in a large tent as part of the 1979 International Caravan Festival in Toronto. Mrs. Stephenson, the president of the Women's Committee of the Company, had invited me to sing at this fund-raising event to benefit the COC. A pretty young woman with long black hair and large luminous eyes selling beer and peanuts caught my attention as soon as I entered the tent. After ordering my free beer, I asked for pea-nuts, and she asked for payment. My admission ticket only allowed for one free drink, she told me. I pushed for the free peanuts only as a pre-text to flirt shamelessly with her, but she ignored my attentions. I asked Mrs. Stephenson if she knew the young woman. She smiled but shrugged her shoulders, having noticed our little act. On stage, I sat on a stool and sang Charlie Chaplin's "Smile," my outpouring of energies entirely posi-tive, yet the young woman, busy serving drinks, wouldn't look my way. I stopped singing halfway and called on her to bring me my peanuts, or I'd stop singing. She stood impassive for an instant as if to dare me until Mrs. Stephenson shoved a bag of peanuts into her hand and pushed her towards the stage. I took her hand and finished the song looking directly into her eyes, but she remained impassive. After my number, she walked away, and I couldn't get her attention anymore.

I returned a second night without being asked. This time I sang what had become my signature aria, The Toreador Song. The young woman was still there, but selling balloons this time. She pretended not to notice me or my singing, but I could feel sparks flying all around her. I played the same trick as the night before, stopped in the middle of my aria, and asked her to bring me a red balloon. She broke a timid smile, and I fell suddenly in love with my second Prima Donna. This time I wanted to pursue her without playing games. I asked Mrs. Stephenson to formally introduce us. She smiled as she walked me over to her, "Meet my daughter, Kathryn," she said.

Whether it was the song or my white suit and hat or my large smile, the young woman handing out balloons let me drive her home. That was the start of my life-long relationship with Kathryn Stephenson.

Kathryn was all I wanted in a woman. Before we met, she had spent time in Europe and carried herself with a certain air of sophistication and self-assurance, even if she looked younger than her tender twenty years. I was highly attracted to her physically. Her piercing black eyes, thick dark hair and porcelain skin exuded youthful energy and purity. To top it all off, she came from an opera-loving family, played the piano and the violin, and studied music therapy at York University.

We had an intense summer romance before I had to return to Paris to follow a prerequisite program at the École d'Art Lyrique of Paris to be coached in French repertoire and French diction in preparation for being signed at the Paris Opera.

Before leaving for my new adventure, I played a role in a COC production of *Simon Boccanegra* singing alongside my father, I as Paolo, my father as Boccanegra. The press covered the father-son angle, and I was excited about my first unique singing experience next to my father. The expectations were challenging enough, then I broke an ankle dancing in Kathryn's living room, and I was afraid I'd have to cancel the performance. The angels were on my side during this period, and the cast on my ankle and the limp it caused, rather than hinder me in my role, helped me better impersonate the role of Paolo—a man older than I was then. Sherrill Milnes, the acclaimed American dramatic baritone, came from New York for the opening and congratulated me backstage after the performance on both my acting and my voice.

In Paris for my studies, I missed Kathryn terribly. The walls were paper-thin in my tiny single bedroom in La Cité Universitaire, and I could hear all goings-on in the next room. Every morning I would wake up to cockroaches on the walls, and I would try to kill them with my slippers. My food consisted of a baguette and a huge chunk of *pâté*, which I kept on my window ledge to keep it fresh. I would sometimes splurge and buy myself a *petite suisse* for dessert. I had Kathryn's picture beside my bed in and I would go to sleep looking at her and dream about her.

She joined me for a magical Christmas holiday. My bleak living conditions gave her a taste of what life in Paris would be like for an aspiring artist. We were a young couple in love in Paris. Ours was a romantic story, and we loved each other dearly from the very start.

The left side of my brain tried to dissuade me from jumping into another marriage so soon after the dismal end of the first one, yet I wanted Kathryn with me all the time. In my heart, I believed that our relationship was solid and meant to last. The more time I spent with her, the more I saw a warm and loving woman, a good woman with a big heart, and I knew that she would be the mother of my children. The official proposal would come soon but not as romantically as she had probably expected.

In the new year, before moving permanently to Paris, I joined my parents in New York to see my father sing in Verdi's *Un Ballo in Maschera* with Luciano Pavarotti conducted by Giuseppe Patané. Both my parents loved Kathryn, and I brought her with me. After the performance, the Met management held an exclusive reception for the ensemble and their spouses at 21 Club. At a certain point in the evening, Maestro Patané joined Kathryn and me, and I introduced Kathryn as my fiancée, without paying much attention to what the word fiancée implies. We were not engaged officially.

With glass in hand, he congratulated us and asked, "So, when are you getting married?

"I haven't asked her yet," I said embarrassed.

"Well, ask her now," he joked. "What are you waiting for?"

Without losing a beat and looking at Kathryn, I said, "Will you marry me in May?" Kathryn looked on astonished and smiled demurely.

Sensing a gaffe and insensitivity, I pulled her aside at the first chance I got, "May is a perfectly fine month to get married," I explained. "Will you marry me?"

"Yes," she said, "but that was not very romantic."

To me, it felt very romantic. We left the party and walked hand in hand on brightly lit West 52nd Street in the heart of midtown Manhattan, making plans for our new life in Paris and the many possibilities before for us. My parents had also proclaimed their young love in New York, she en route to Paris; he to Rome. I kept my promise. Back home, I bought a beautiful ring. We were engaged in February and planned to marry in May. Sadly, just one month after our engagement tragedy struck Kathryn's family with the untimely death of her father. Both families agreed we should still proceed with the wedding plans. We opted for a small but elegant reception.. Paris would be my wedding present to Kathryn.

Chapter 26
L'Opéra de Paris:
The Start of a Career

Paris and a beautiful wife, I had finally made it! Too soon after the family tragedy, Kathryn left her mother, two sisters, and a brother with a heavy heart. I hoped the City of Light would restore her bright outlook towards life, a look I'd seen in her luminous eyes when we first met. As for me, I was fully committed to my new responsibilities. The first role I sang brought me great critical reviews as a new up-and-coming baritone. My mother came from Toronto to help prepare me for Morris Townsend's role in *L'Héritière,* an opera based on the Henry James novel *Washington Square.* Already, there was a Hollywood film adaptation starring Olivia de Havilland and Montgomery Clift. Strangely enough, I had seen the movie as a young boy and loved Clift's acting. I based my interpretation on his bravado and was honoured to meet Henry James's great-niece, who came to the opening night. My father also flew in for the premiere, and at the end of the performance, backstage, he watched me with a satisfied look as I conducted myself with the dressers and stage crew.

Then he said to me, "Gino, what you did was incredible. You should have been born before me; I would have learned from you." Those words were like beautiful music to my ears. That's how things were in our family in those early days as my career was beginning and my father's was maturing. We attended each other's important performances and supported and rooted for each other.

One minor drama that unfolded during the following performances of this new Paris adventure is that I had no understudy; I was the only singer who could perform the role. During the two-week run, I caught severe bronchitis and felt the pressure of looming cancellation for the first time in my career. I had to decide the night before the show to give the director time to inform and refund patrons. In this situation, an internal battle with oneself takes place, hoping that you can magically get better. After much struggle, I decided to cancel. It was a horrible feeling, but I learned a lesson about protecting my integrity. Better to lose a performance and accompanying pay than to sing badly at one. Reviews were mind-boggling and excellent for the following performances.

The French critics wrote that the only person they could understand in the opera was me. My studies at the École d'Art Lyrique had worked wonders; my diction in French was pitch-perfect. The French public also loved my version of André Messager's *Véronique* at the Opera Comique. I understood this to be the turning point in my career. From then on, critics began to associate me with French Opera.

For this recognition, I owe a debt of appreciation to Bernard Lefort, a VIP in the opera world then, who gave me my big break in Europe. He was the new general director of the Paris Opera when he came to Quebec to hear some new young singers, and he offered me a three-year contract on the spot, based on one audition. Later, he gave me a big boost of confidence when I read what he wrote about me in a book on opera, *Opera, mon métier*:

> I just found someone... if he trusts me, he will be the greatest baritone of his generation; he is Quilico's son Gino. He has fantastic assets: he is very handsome, and his voice is disarmingly natural like that of his father... I have never seen anyone have so much intelligence, and already have a vocal technique that is completely safe. He worked with his father and offers, musically speaking, very varied things: he sings Hamlet and Don Juan without the songs being alike. It is superb..."

Bernard Lefort took on the role of Pygmalion and was determined to groom me as he had done for José Van Dam, but unlike Van Dam, I already had an extensive repertoire, thanks to my parents' training. Together with my father, Lefort set out a course of action. According to them, I should go easy and not accept any roles other than *Don*

Giovanni, *Manon*, and *Don Pasquale* until the age of thirty, slowly adding *Don Carlos*, *Les Pêcheurs de Perles*, and *Mireille*. Only after age 35 should I tackle the more demanding *Rigoletto* and other great Verdi operas. I was twenty-five at the time, and ten years seemed like a very long time to wait, but I was determined to keep to the schedule.

Kathryn had loved the idea of coming to Paris with me, or maybe it was the romanticized idea that many people have of the city. Visiting Paris as a tourist and living in the city day by day are two very different experiences. She was born and had grown up in protective polite Toronto society, and from the beginning, found the ways of Parisians brusque, unfriendly, and even aggressive. She was mourning her father, and the sadness she had brought with her resurfaced now and then. I understood the reasons: she was far from home for a longer period of time than ever before. On top of missing her family, she was only 21 and spoke little French.

Our first living conditions were probably a notch or two below that of Marcello, Rodolfo, and Mimi in *La Bohème*. Our closet-sized room had one single bed and no toilet but many cockroaches to keep us company. After jousting for space in the single bed, we took to putting a thin mattress on the floor where I slept so Kathryn could have the bed to herself. On nights before an audition or a performance, Kathryn offered to sleep on the floor so I could get a good night's rest. Then we graduated into a fifth-floor apartment with a shower. Still, we could only use the much-appreciated amenity tucked into a tiny closet one at a time, and we only ever got three minutes' worth of precious hot water. One sink in the room served for brushing our teeth, washing dishes, shampooing our hair. With one weak heater in the living room, we huddled in bed to keep warm. The first year in Paris, I got sick at least five times. We both missed the basic comforts we took for granted in Canada, especially a hot bath. But we were young and tried to laugh about it. I was away from the tiny apartment all day, and I took all the inconveniences in stride, part and parcel of an opera singer's growing career, ones I had experienced or heard about as a child.

I sensed Kathryn's discomfort and even felt guilty at times for not being able to offer her more. But artistic success didn't equate with financial success during that first phase of my career, and I didn't want to count on my parents to help me out after they had covered my first wedding, a divorce, and a second wedding. This time, I wanted to do it on my own.

My days were full, studying new operas and making new connections in the European music community. Kathryn didn't have the same opportunities for making new friends as I did. But we found surrogate parents, Monsieur et Madame Giffard who lived in a posh apartment in Saint-Germain-des-Prés. Madame Giffard ran an exclusive tapestry store in that same area. With wealthy clients from around the world she had a sophisticated circle of friends. I had known the Giffards from my childhood days in Paris when I attended school with their son Olivier, and my sister was friends with their daughter Anne. After we had left the city, my family had hosted Olivier in Rome and New York. When I returned to Paris, I reconnected with Olivier. As adults, we did not have many common interests, and we didn't see much of each other, but his parents invited Kathryn and me over every weekend for much appreciated French home-cooking.

They also invited us to their home near Carpentras in Provence several times. Kathryn loved it there. The beautiful stone house with a huge pool was built on a hill and encircled with cherry trees. We had never seen cherries dangling from tree branches like clusters of sparkling rubies illuminated by the sun. We would climb the trees and eat the cherries as we picked them. The first time we ate so many that we had tummy aches. The Giffards hosted an eclectic crowd of fascinating guests in their stone-walled dining room with its vaulted ceiling and authentic French Provençal furniture. It was Provence living at its best. At times, we would visit the rest of the region on our own and picnic with a bottle of wine, cheese, and baguette.

During our first year in Paris, we took every opportunity to enjoy what the city had to offer two young people in love. We attended concerts, the ballet, and despite our semi-squalid living conditions, splurged at many great restaurants in the city and countryside.

It bothered me to see Kathryn at times still looking sad and forlorn. Though engaged in these new experiences, she still had trouble making friends, likely because of the language barrier. I did wish for her to find her own direction, passion, and interests, but life was centered around me and my career, and it must have felt one-sided for her.

To avoid staying alone all day in the claustrophobic apartment, Kathryn accompanied me to all my rehearsals. She had sung in a choir, studied music, and, as a young girl, had aspired to be a singer. She took a keen interest in my roles. After each rehearsal, we discussed what worked and didn't work in my performances. We didn't always agree, and we often argued, but having her by my side boosted my self-confidence. After all, I was just a twenty-five-year-old opera singer upon which huge expectations had been placed, a long distance from the security I had felt with my parents, especially my mother. At times, all the hype about me scared me more than it pleased me.

I also brought Kathryn along on outings with my friends, and I tried to cheer her with my enthusiasm and behind-the-scene stories.

L'Opéra de Paris at the time was badly in need of repair. I experienced a bizarre prank at the Opera meant as a protest for the dismal conditions performers had to endure, but about which the general public was unaware. Unfortunately, it was Monserrat Caballé, that bore the brunt of the joke. During one of my earliest performances of *Turandot*, with the diva, someone threw two live chickens with their feet tied from the lighting truss. The chickens died on impact, and poor Monserrat had to walk around the chickens as she posed Turandot's famous three riddles: "What is born each night and dies at dawn? What flickers red and warms like a flame yet is not fire? What is like ice yet burns?" These questions are so tricky that no man could solve and thus claim the right to marry her. They are also deep and poetic. What must have Monserrat thought to keep her composure as she walked around the chickens? When the stage crew ran up to check, they found a bag of excrement tied to a bunch of long-stemmed roses, most probably meant to be thrown down on the diva while she made her last bow.

Part of my optimism came from the excellent roles alongside many other great singers. I remember fondly my role of Ned Keene in *Peter Grimes* with Jon Vickers, who took both Kathryn and me under his wing, giving me valuable suggestions and even taking us to dinners. He insisted on calling Kathryn Kate. He took me out to lunch one day during our rehearsals to a bistro close to the opera house. We both had a huge plate of mussels. He sat in front of me and, as usual, gave me valuable advice but, in the same breath, also mentioned that if anyone ever crossed him, he'd get back at them viciously. I immediately made a mental note of this warning and told myself I better not upset this man. He seemed to be paranoid! Then I recalled when we had first crossed paths. I was singing in the chorus at the National Arts Centre in Ottawa in *The Queen of Spades*. Jon almost took my head off one night. He threw a drinking glass backward after his big aria. The drinking glass went flying past my head.

A few years after *Peter Grimes* and our lunch, I sang in *I Pagliacci* with him, and this time he had to kill me with a large switchblade knife. As it often happens in opera, they had assigned two singers for the role. I was the first cast, but the second baritone singing my part got his hand badly cut by the famous knife. Jon had been clear during that famous meal: if you cross me, you may come straight to me in open arms, but at the last minute, I'll find a way to turn my wrist and punch you in the gut. I had been warned, but not the other baritone. Maybe he had done or said something that displeased Jon? I performed with Jon Vickers three times in my life. Every time, I remembered I was putting my life into Jon's hands if, somehow, I had inadvertently done something to disappoint him.

My salary increased by 33% each year, living conditions improved accordingly, and we moved to a more comfortable apartment in the 17th arrondissement. My contract also allowed me to take jobs outside the Paris Opera and at music venues in other countries. Contrary to the earlier admonition from Bernard Lefort not to tackle too much in the first years, I didn't refuse too many invitations. It meant time spent away from the home we had made, though Kathryn accompanied me on many of my trips. We travelled to Italy, Spain, Germany, and England, mostly for my performances, but we were together and took every opportunity to visit all the sights and met some incredible people in the music field. I also took contracts in Washington, D.C., and Montreal. Depending on the length of these contracts in North America, Kathryn accompanied me, and the trips gave her the much-needed opportunity to visit with her family as well.

I was in Edinburgh in 1982, singing in *Manon Lescaut* for the Festival, when we found out Kathryn was pregnant. She glowed with beauty and happiness. Things seemed to be looking up for us, and I felt more assured and secure than ever. Whenever I auditioned for any roles I was uncertain about, I followed my father's advice, "When you feel nervous about an audition, look straight into the eyes of those in front of you and tell yourself, 'Not one of them can do what I am doing.'"

I auditioned successfully for Sir John Tooley at Covent Garden, who booked me for my debut role of Valentin in *Faust* for the following year singing next to Alfredo Kraus, the distinguished *bel canto* Spanish tenor.

Meanwhile in Paris, the pace of work intensified, especially after Alain Lanceron, the artistic advisor of Patty Marconi of French EMI, invited me to record *Manon*, launching my recording and film career. I remember the in-studio session as one of the most painful experiences, not for any usual artistic conflicts or insecurities, but for a very embarrassing condition to which not even opera stars are immune: I suffered from severe bleeding hemorrhoids during the entire recording. It was a serious a condition that had also plagued my father and his father and had, at times, left me weak and debilitated from the loss of blood. I would be recording all day and spending the rest of the time at night in cold baths to help with the pain and inflammation. Luckily it wasn't in front of my usual audience, and I didn't have to restrain my pained expression, but I may have padded my role with more emotion and passion than it demanded. Bernard Lefort had given me my first important break; Alain Lanceron, my second with the recording of *Manon*. After that, I was as busy recording arias as I was performing on stage. I did 28 other recordings over the next few years.

I had difficulty saying no to the various projects coming my way, and the summer that Kathryn was pregnant proved frantic and chaotic, both professionally and personally. The weather was sweltering, and Kathryn, in the early months of her pregnancy, experienced constant nausea in our non-air-conditioned apartment. One day, she came home crying and pale. She had gone for a walk and, in the heat and humidity, lost consciousness and collapsed on the sidewalk close to our apartment. No one stopped to help her. Even the mail delivery lady who surely must have recognized her, walked right past Kathryn leaving her to get up and stagger her way back to the apartment by herself. Luckily, it had been a soft fall, and she wasn't hurt, but she was shattered by the indifference shown to her by the locals.

"I was treated like a homeless person," she cried. "I have become invisible. No matter how well I dress, no matter how hard I try to speak the language, I'll never be treated like I belong here."

I was overtaken by anguish to see her crying and holding her slightly distended belly as if to protect the life growing inside. I was also exhausted and could not offer her more than some inane expression of comfort, "Who cares about these snobby Parisians on the street when we are the toast of the town and travelling all over Europe?"

"Easy for you to talk and laugh things up, as usual. You have your career. What do I have?"

That comment pierced my heart. I understood that her life goals were not advancing as well as mine. She had quit her studies in music therapy to marry me. She had by now learned to speak a nearly perfect French, yet she still felt treated like an outsider and unlike me, she had no career of her own to look forward to for all her troubles. It hurt me to know that Paris had not turned out to be the dream I had promised her, despite all my efforts, but I just didn't know what to do. I had to follow the course I had set out for myself, and Paris is where it had landed me.

Life was not as painless for me as it seemed, and I had to develop my own coping mechanism. Even when I grappled with self-doubt and frustrations, I handled the pressures with outward humour and laughter to ease tensions, giving the impression that nothing bothered me. This attitude often backfired because it also gave people the impression that I took my work and life in general too lightly. Nothing could be further from the truth. Does anyone really understand how hard an opera singer has to work to make it all look so easy?

Preparing for one opera is demanding work; learning four to six different operas simultaneously as I was doing saps every minute of your day, your energy, and all of your thoughts. I'd be preparing for my current performance while also studying for the ones coming up the next year and the year after. Singing a foreign language like Russian in Tchaikovsky's *Eugene Onegin* and *The Queen of Spades* or German in Strauss's *Die Fledermaus*, required hours of meticulous study. I had to learn the correct pronunciation and the meaning of the words to properly express them in the music. And I also had to learn my partner's words sung to me. *Onegin* took two years of diligent work with three different Russian pianists in Milan and London, until finally, I got it right in San Francisco, where Susanna Lemberskaya patiently taught me the phonetics of the Russian language.

Once I memorized the music, the text, and the technique, I researched other singers who had tackled the same roles, listening to them on CD, if available, or attending live performances if I happened to be in a city where they were performing. Then I would do a character study of the role I was to interpret and read about the opera's historical period. At times, I read inspirational books on how to identify my inner self to help me find my persona's essence and true character.

First-day rehearsals and meetings with the other singers, the maestro, and stage directors brought along other pressures. I had to determine if their versions or views on the operatic role for which I had studied so diligently were different from my own. This often resulted in clashes over perspective about the characters, music, or movements on stage. I was always very well-prepared and able to offer suggestions. Sometimes the troupe would accept my ideas, but other times, they challenged them vehemently. Three to six weeks of exhausting rehearsal with the other performers, who often had their own large egos, could be incredibly stimulating but could also prove boring or downright hostile. The psychological aspect of handling all the pressure during the run of the performance and still concentrate on the singing could be nerve-racking. To keep sane, I told myself that I was lucky to be doing what I had wanted to do. I tried to live by my father's credo, "I am not paid to work, but rather I am paid to be happy." I looked for the rosier side of things, tried not to dwell on the negative, put on a happy face even though inside I was a ball of nerves.

After the youthful enthusiasm of the first years in Paris, I felt constantly torn between my growing career and Kathryn's wellbeing. I was still hopeful that as our fortunes improved, so would Kathryn's sense of contentment. I didn't see my parents much during this period except the few times when Father performed in Europe, but I kept in constant touch with them by phone and in long letters to my mother. She was the only person in whom I could confide my insecurities and fears, including my inability to ease Kathryn's unhappiness in Paris.

"Pace yourself," she wrote that summer in response to my complaints of being tired and overwhelmed. "Don't overreach until you feel ready. You're still very young. Try to find some equilibrium between career and home life. It's the key to appreciating the value of what's really important."

I tried to heed her words, but as my reputation grew as a baritone with a high lyrical voice, I was in demand all over Europe, and every offer seemed crucial to expanding my repertoire and experience. I'd be singing *The Barber of Seville* in Toulouse, then back to Paris for *Romeo and Juliet*, then off to Salzburg for Rossini's *La Cenerentola*, and back in Paris for *Turandot*. But an ugly dark presence was beginning to raise its shadow over me again. The sense of fear and foreboding initiated not from some imaginary being but from the violence happening all over Europe, especially in France and England, where I sang.

Chapter 27
Explosions

Kathryn and I left our apartment in an upbeat mood on an early September morning, on our way to Orly airport. After a heavy summer of frantic work and humid weather, I welcomed the crisp fall air and the gentle sunshine. She was four months pregnant and was leaving to spend some time with her family in Toronto. I promised to join her for Christmas. I hated seeing Kathryn leaving alone in her condition, but my schedule didn't allow me any personal time until December. The following day I was to meet the great conductor Hebert von Karajan in Berlin, where we would record *Carmen* together under the direction of the Berlin Philarmonic Orchestra. Two weeks after the recording, I would fly to Glasgow to sing in *Manon Lescaut*, then on to Dallas for *I Pagliacci*. My agent had set the schedule three years in advance, and I could not change it on a whim.

After seeing Kathryn off, I waited at the airport for some two hours for the arrival of my friend Neil Shicoff and his wife from New York. They would be staying at my apartment as our guests while we were away and he performed in *Eugene Onegin* at the Paris Opera.

"They'll soon charge me rent at the airport," I jokingly told Neil. The Orly airport had become more familiar to me than the building on Rue Cardinet, in the 17th Arrondissement, where we now lived. After two years in Paris, our living conditions had significantly improved.

The 17th Arrondissement, also known as Batignolles-Monceau, together with the 16th Arrondissement and the nearby *commune* of Neuilly-sur-Seine, formed one of the most affluent and prestigious neighbourhoods in the whole of France. It housed the Palais des Congrès of Paris and its adjoining Hôtel Concorde La Fayette and many foreign embassies. The large Bois de Boulogne public park, with lakes and bucolic gardens, was a short drive away, and I often accompanied Kathryn there on summer weekends for a respite from the heat.

I was happy to see Neil, and we laughed in the car as we exchanged stories and the latest gossip in the opera world. I first met Neil, who is a few years older than me, in Cincinnati when he was already well-established in his career. I was young, inexperienced, and in the thrall of my first wife's caprices and the scuffles that followed. I had barely had time to become acquainted with Neil after telling him how much I admired his sweet, lyrical voice and dramatic stage presence before I ran away from that place. I met him again in Ottawa, where he sang with my father in *Rigoletto*—again a brief connection. Neil, like me, had also followed in his father's footsteps. The older Shicoff, Sidney, was a respected and renowned cantor in New York.

Neil and I became real friends at the Paris Opera when we sang in Gounod's *Romeo and Juliet*, Neil as Romeo, I as Mercurio, and Barbara Hendricks as Juliet. I forged two life-long friendships in that production with Neil and Barbara. The three of us have spent many good times encouraging each other and helping one another through difficulties in our careers. Neil and I have spent some crazy nights playing cards when performing together in several productions, including *Romeo and Juliet*, *La Bohème*, and *Carmen*. We have crossed paths all over the world. When we're together, it is as if we have never been apart, then we go our separate ways and may not see each other again for years. We speak from time to time on the phone, but we understand each other well and don't need to keep in touch about trivial things. We are honest and straightforward with each other. Our common ground is our love for singing, and we have each other's backs when we work together.

I dropped the couple off at our apartment, and was driving off to park the car when suddenly the ground shook as an explosive boom shattered the silence. I hit the brakes. Some 100 metres or less away from me, a car exploded in smoke and rose several feet up into the air. Shattered glass dropped all over the place like sparks from a firework display, followed by a surreal silence. I froze inside my car, confused and scared, staring at the bombed car parked right across from a school, the Lycée Carnot, and the Israeli consulate. The shocked silence was soon broken by screams and shouts, and people running desperately towards the school. I finally got out of the car and started running towards the burning vehicle to see if I could help, but then I froze again in fear of another explosion. I was paralyzed, not knowing what to do. People running out of nearby buildings asked questions, but they were afraid to approach the car like me.

Neil and his wife appeared next to me, seemingly out of nowhere, with fear in their eyes. A woman, the superintendent of my building, ran towards us screaming, « Mes enfants, mes enfants! ». Before I could speak to her, she ran into the school. I knew her two children studied there. The glass from the school's windows had blown inwards, and now children and adults walked out with blood smeared on their hands and faces. It is a moment frozen in time that I will never forget.

We tried to reassure the people around us and calm them down, but for me, the scene of the explosion kept replaying itself in my head. I'm not sure how much time passed until I heard the wailing of sirens and saw emergency vehicles arrive. The police blocked the street and asked us to leave the scene. Finally, I parked the car and checked on the building superintendent before joining Neil and his wife in the apartment. Thankfully, her children were safe with her. Neil and I poured ourselves a few stiff drinks to bring us back to reality. We were so pumped up with nervous energy neither of us could sit still. With all the adrenalin running through my body, only scotch could bring me down and lower my heartbeat.

I called Toronto to let Mrs. Stephenson know that I was okay, in case she heard about the bombing on the news. I caught her just as she was on her way to the airport to pick up Kathryn. The thought that I could have driven by the explosion with Kathryn in the car had her flight been scheduled later made my body shake again. As I prepared my bags for my trip to Berlin, the sound of the explosion and the many scenarios of what could have happened kept repeating themselves. What if I had been driving a little faster or not braked suddenly? I would have passed right by the car, which meant I would have received the full force of the explosion. And what if the bomb had detonated earlier with Kathryn and baby in the car? Three lives and all my dreams and hopes blown up in one blast of smoke!

We later learned that the targeted car, a Peugeot 504, belonged to an Israeli diplomat, Amos Manel. The Lebanese Armed Revolutionary Factions (FARL) claimed responsibility for the bomb as an anti-Israeli act of terrorism. There had been three people in the car: the diplomat, and his aunt and uncle visiting Paris., The three were seriously injured but they miraculously survived Fortunately, none of the Lycée children were killed, though more than fifty were wounded and certainly left terrified and scarred. Had the bomb exploded only a few minutes later, at the end of the school day with hundreds of students rushing out of the building, it would have resulted in a more tragic bloodshed. The bombing happened on the eve of Rosh Hashanah, a few months after the Israeli invasion of Lebanon. Among other previous attacks, the FARL had assassinated American lieutenant colonel Charles Ray in January and Israeli diplomat Yacov Barsimantov in April. Both were shot dead in Paris.

These other incidents, though tragic, had only been news items for me till then, but the aftershock, the confusion, and fear from what I had witnessed persisted for months as I went about my daily routine. Only once on stage did I completely erase them from my consciousness.

The morning after the attack, I was still feeling shaken while waiting for a taxi to the airport. The bomb scene was now calm and free of debris. I closed my eyes as the cab drove by it. Once on the plane, I tried to erase the concrete details of the bomb attack as I mentally prepared for my role of Dancaïre. The thought of meeting the great Maestro Herbert von Karajan along with the tenor José Carreras and mezzo-soprano Agnes Baltsa energized me.

I had spent my whole salary for the recording with Deutsche Grammophon to stay at the famous Hotel Kempinski. On my arrival at the luxury hotel, I started vocalizing in the shower before meeting von Karajan that evening. I didn't realize how loudly I was singing until the phone in the bathroom rang, and I heard the courteous but firm voice of the receptionist, "*Guten Tag, Herr* Quilico. Mr. von Karajan thinks you have a good voice, but he is trying to have his afternoon siesta."

Embarrassed, I was all hyped up and could not relax, so I decided to go down to the pool. An attendant dressed in white greeted me with a broad smile and asked, "*Guten Tag*, sauna or pool?" I chose the sauna, thinking it more relaxing, and peacefully walked in naked and sat on the cedar wood bench with my eyes closed. After a few minutes, I sensed someone walking in. I opened my eyes, and a drop-dead gorgeous, naked girl walked in and smiled at me with a *"Guten Tag!"* I immediately jumped up. Did the attendant send in the girl for me? He had a curious smile on his face. Was I in the wrong sauna? *"Guten Tag,"* I responded, stood up, covered myself and started walking out, just as an older man and a woman also naked walked in. It finally struck me that Germany must have mixed saunas, but was too embarrassed at my reaction to go back in.

Maestro von Karajan was very gracious when we met later in the evening. "Hope you had a chance to rest after all that vocalizing," he said with a smile.

"Yes, they have a wonderful sauna," I said.

To this day, I can't help but chuckle to myself whenever I walk into a sauna.

On my return to Paris before leaving for Dallas, I passed by the scene of the terrorist attack several times. I touched the stone walls full of holes and felt fresh fear in my bones. I did it intentionally to help myself get over the anxiety that often assaulted me but remained unspoken. It was a sickening feeling every time. In retrospect, I had had a nervous shock but had neglected to treat it. The workings of the human brain are a strange thing. Evil forces lay dormant, surfacing from time to time to play tricks on my sense of security, yet I failed to acknowledge the source. What had happened to the self-confidence and devil-may-care attitude I had enjoyed as a younger man at the start of my career? I wondered. My mood and spirit swung from elation to despair from one day to the next, conditioned by external events out of my control and the roles that I performed. I kept my fears to myself. I now had a wife and child to take care of and an image of bravura and strength to preserve. As time went on, I often felt as if I was forever playing a role, whether on stage or off.

From Dallas, I flew directly to Toronto for a Canadian Christmas with Kathryn and the family and a well-deserved rest. Together we returned to Paris in January in great anticipation for the birth of our baby while 1983 promised to be packed with scheduled performances: *Die Fledermaus* in Paris, *I Pagliacci* in the Canary Islands, a recording of *Romeo and Juliet* in Toulouse, *La Bohème* in Florence, *Manon* in Montreal, *Faust* in London.

Chapter 28
Enrico

None of the expectations I had for 1983 equaled the joy I felt in February at the birth of my son, Enrico. I was singing the male leading role, Eisenstein, in *Die Fledermaus* by Richard Strauss when Kathryn was hospitalized for observation and a possible premature induced birth. She was as nervous about being left alone as by the procedure, We had a large private room on the top floor of the private Clinique La Muette, where they set up a second bed for me beside my wife. They made an exception about visiting hours, and I could arrive at any time of day or night because they knew I was singing at the Paris Opera.

The operetta itself, *Die Fledermaus*, so full of entertaining and comic moments, left me feeling joyful and in great spirits. As soon as I took my last bow, I rushed to the clinic. Fortunately Enrico arrived in the early morning and I was able to welcome him to the world and embrace an exhausted Kathryn after a breach birth The following evening, I went on stage with a pocket full of cigars.

Earlier on the first night of the performance, something of a minor scandal had occurred. Strauss, who is best known for his ballroom pieces, based his operetta on a popular French vaudeville comedy, but in the translation, the librettists substituted the bawdy French *réveillon* scene with a ballroom setting, maybe to cater to the more elevated tastes of the Viennese audience. In this new Paris production, the director went all out to transform the masked ballroom scene into a farcical French orgy. The Paris Opera Ballet Company dancers wore bodysuits that made them look nude though no specific body parts were exposed. The choreography was excellent, yet the Parisian audience, to everyone's surprise, gave the dance number a tremendous boo. The reviewers also disapproved of the new interpretation and pronounced the ballroom scene distasteful. Hard to believe, I thought, that the city that gave the world the Folies Bergère would find this type of semi-nudity offensive. The Ballet Company was just as offended by the audience's and the reviewers' negative reaction, and they refused to perform the next show. I had heard repeatedly that the French audience could be harsh and led easily to booing, but excited and worried about the impending birth, I didn't pay much attention to this rising crisis. The director must have had the same thought as I had, for when we went on stage the night following my son's birth, I found the Folies Bergère dancers backstage wearing even fewer clothes than the regular company dancers and no bodysuits. We had never even rehearsed with them. In my jubilant mood and surrounded by this circus-like atmosphere, I figured I could improvise and get away with it. In Act II, during the masked ball scene, when everyone was not what they were supposed to be and playing wicked tricks on one another, I ramped up the actions of the super excited character of Eisenstein. I ran around the dancers on stage, handing out cigars without losing a beat in my singing. The singers played along with big smiles on their faces, patting me on the shoulder. After one of the tenors sang out, "*Cet un garçon!*" the audience applauded. I bowed and threw the remaining cigars at them. It was one of the few applauses of the evening because they also booed the Folies Bergère dancers. For me, the evening had been a euphoric and joyous moment in keeping with the opera and my supercharged emotions. I later told Kathryn that if Oscars were awarded to opera singers my acting that night would have garnered me one of those golden statues.

Because of the breach birth, Kathryn stayed at the hospital for a week and I slept in the room with her every night. Some evenings after the performance, some of my fellow ensemble singers came to the clinic with me, and we sang in the large room for Kathryn and her very appreciative nurses. On stage, the ballroom number farce continued. The Folies Bergère dancers, greatly offended by the jeers, refused to return.

The company dancers had to be coaxed back and continued to be booed every night. I laughed it all off. The show must go on, we say, and it did.

The doctors and nurses at the hospital were very kind to me. They allowed me to set a stereo in the room overlooking the rooftops of Paris. I played Mozart for my son and Kathryn. It was winter and cold, and it reminded me of the set in *La Bohème,* but I felt blessed. As a boy, I had gone looking for Cinecittà on my bike, dreaming of the magic life of a movie star. Many fairy-tale events in one's life happen without the help of movie cameras and are then played over and over again in one's memory.

While at the hospital, we discussed names for the baby, thinking that, as in North America, we'd have plenty of time after leaving the hospital to settle on one. Then, on the set, one of the backstage crew members told me that a baby's name needs to be registered within a week by French law. I panicked and ran to the register's office. When I joined Kathryn to pick her up and take her home, I announced that I had just registered our son as Enrico Luigi Gino Quilico: Enrico after a character I had played in *Lucia di Lammermoor,* only because I liked the sound of the name. Luigi was for my grandfather and father, and Gino, of course, for me. Kathryn was infuriated that I had done this without consulting her, even though she liked the name and it was one we had considered. I promised her she'd have complete freedom to name our second child. That, too, did not go over well. After a breach birth with forceps, she was hardly looking forward to a second one.

Chapter 29
The Nomad Life

For a while, I lived on a high, all fears and doubts dissipating in the glow of fatherhood and professional success. A few months later, in Canada, I had the great honour of singing with my father for Queen Elizabeth II to celebrate the repatriation of the Canadian Constitution. It proved to be one of those events about which, as a family, we liked to tease Father. The organizers had instructed us on protocol and not to address the Queen unless spoken to or to extend a hand to her unless she did so first. Well, of course, my gregarious father did not obey orders. When the Queen arrived, he extended his hand and said, "Hello." The Queen seemed pleasantly surprised and laughed. Prince Phillip immediately jumped in and laughed as well, saying, "I remember you." My father had met them before at another event in British Columbia and most likely had committed the same blunder.

My calendar was full for the next three years. In December of that same year, I flew to London for a meeting with a British agent. My debut at Covent Garden in *Faust* had garnered some glowing reviews. I considered moving to London for the sake of Kathryn, who was still quite miserable in Paris. Enrico was not yet a year old. I stopped by Harrods to look for Christmas presents to bring back to Kathryn and the baby. I had not quite shrugged off the darkness of the *Faust* opera, but later as I walked the busy street crowded with Christmas shoppers, I remember feeling the sense of cheerfulness that English Victorian Christmas decorations and music can elicit even in the most cynical of people. Then, once again, the boom of a terrifying explosion shook my fragile mental state.

It happened not right in front of me as in Paris, but close enough, at the Harrods entrance I had walked by only fifteen minutes earlier. The bomb killed three members of the public and three police officers in an instant. The IRA later admitted it had planted the bomb. I asked myself: was someone sending me a message, and from where does this evil that hurts and kills innocent people come?

After London, the strain and the earlier feelings of dread and depression I had felt in Cincinnati and Paris intensified. Terrorist attacks in Paris had been constant since the early 80s, and the IRA in England had also attacked before. Still, after seeing a car go up in flames right in front of me and witnessing Christmas shoppers blown up in plain sight, I became jittery and anxious, outright paranoid as I went about my daily life. At times, I would get on my hands and knees to look under my car for suspicious objects before turning the ignition. I felt nervous walking between parked cars and would jump at the slightest sudden noise.

Worse than the fear of physical harm, I also suffered from the fear of accomplishment. Would I always be able to give one hundred percent to my art? How far could I go before breaking down? Europe loomed large, offering boundless possibilities, but it was also a dangerous place for someone who had experienced the haunting fears of dangerous presences.

I wrote to my mother, "I have been terribly depressed. I don't really know why, but I seem to have lost some of my confidence. Maybe it has to do with my nearing my thirties...." I still tried not to exaggerate my dark state of mind, not to worry her unnecessarily, so I signed off in a lighter tone, "So this is your son signing off with a bad case of mind rot brought on by the green fog. What is the green fog, you ask? It's like a silent, creepy, smelly fart that infests the whole room the minute it walks in."

She responded, "Worried about nearing thirty? Do you realize how much you have achieved already? Don't be so hard on yourself. Be grateful that you have been given a precious gift, your voice. In turn, it has repaid you with experiences few people can claim. Enjoy Europe while you can, for time passes quickly."

My parents finally found equilibrium after settling in Toronto, and they refused contracts in Europe. I did my best to keep ugly thoughts at bay. I grabbed every opportunity to live the high life while I could. In my free time, when performing outside Paris, I loved driving in my convertible and exploring out-of-the-way places. While in Toulouse in 1984, I explored the Pyrenees, and on a mountain top, I discovered an old castle in ruin, the Château de Montsegur. It amazed and fascinated me because of the sense of mystery and adventure it projected, perched on a precarious rock formation some 1,200 metres above sea level. A year later, I was offered a role in the world premiere of the opera *Montségur* by Marcel Landowski. The story is based on a battle between the Cathars and Catholics fought in the very same castle I visited. The premiere, held in Halle au Grain in Toulouse in 1985-86, had us all dressed up in medieval armour made of real metal mesh, impressive to look at but hot and incredibly uncomfortable to wear.

Despite the discomfort, the costume made me feel like a Sir Lancelot. I truly believe in destiny, and my whole life, I have looked for signs to guide me, whether it's crossing some person's path or moments of déjà vu that leave a strong impression on me. To serendipitously come across a castle that fired my imagination and then a year later to be offered a role in the world premiere of an opera named after that castle was one of those auspicious signs.

Once while in Salzburg, I visited Mozart's house and read the beautiful letter Mozart wrote to his father. It moved me to tears.

Dearest Father, I am not an actor; I am not a dancer. I cannot portray my feelings through body movements; I'm not a mime; I'm not an artist!... but I am a musician, and I can express all those feelings through music.

Mozart has that beautiful, youthful quality in his music that I so much admire and which inspired me at that time. I focused on my career. I wanted to emulate my father and not let my parents down. In 1984, when they told me of an invitation from Montreal's Mayor Jean Drapeau to perform as a family at a sports arena, I was busy recording the role of Mercutio for a new album of Gounod's *Romeo and Juliet*. The concert at the arena didn't mean much to me at the time, but I knew it was significant for my parents, so I flew in two days before for a quick rehearsal with the Maestro, Charles Dutoit, performed the concert, and flew back out. I only understood the importance of that concert after the Montreal audience's incredible outpouring of love and affection for our family and the validation they gave us that evening.

That is what my life was like at that time; I was continuously on the go. After my three-year contract with the Paris Opera was up, I could have renewed it for life, as my father had done at the Met. That would have guaranteed security, but I was restless and revelled in the freedom to sing all over the world. Kathryn's unhappiness in Paris still weighed heavily on me. She had never learned to love Paris, neither in spring, summer, or fall, especially not in winter. I felt she was not with me in spirit as my whirlwind career took me all over the world.

After Enrico's birth, Kathryn felt more acutely the absence of her mother and sisters. "I wish my mother were here," she said wistfully more and more often. I did what I could to help when I was in Paris, and it hurt me to leave her alone with the baby whenever I left. She could no longer travel with me to my performances as in the past and felt more secluded than ever. After three years, she still felt like a foreigner.

With civil unrest in Paris intensifying, the realization that my family may not be safe in that city was one of my constant worries. By Enrico's second birthday, both Kathryn and I wanted another child. I was often invited to London to sing at the Royal Opera House. The "troubles" between the IRA and England remained unresolved, but we did not hear of other terrorist attacks being perpetrated in London. Kathryn persuaded me to move there as a free agent, it being a city where she would feel more at home.

Home base wasn't as important to me as it was to Kathryn since I travelled all over Europe. She was happier in London, though England never inspired me. The constant rain put a damper on my mood, but I had no time to reflect on the reasons why at times, I still felt so downcast. As could be expected, all the travelling and the lack of communication that often comes with constant physical separations began to take a toll on our family life. I felt things start to unravel between Kathryn and me, and I confided in my mother about my problems. She always beseeched me not to let external pressures get in the way of our marriage and to listen to each other's concerns and needs. She wrote, "Try to find some equilibrium between the career and home life. It's the key to appreciating the value of what's really important."

Kathryn and I only lasted a year and a half in London. I felt unsettled and unsatisfied there. It may be my Latin blood, but just as Kathryn had felt out of place in Paris, I now could not get used to the reserve and stuffiness of the Brits, which came across as snobby indifference to me. As an opera singer, I always worried about colds and sore throats. The constant damp English weather put me on edge and in bad moods. My ambivalence about London was also exposing some differences between us. I was open, expansive, and on the go; Kathryn was more closed in, desiring a quieter life.

London did not turn out to be the right compromise for our Mars vs. Venus, yin vs. yang tensions, and with such little time together, our relationship was beginning to feel the strain. I considered settling in sunny Italy, where I had felt happy as a child and from where I could move easily around Europe. When we found out that Kathryn was pregnant again, we had to make some quick and important decisions on where to settle. With a second child coming and me constantly away from home, we felt it best for her to be close to her family in Toronto. As usual, when under mental stress, I shared my thoughts with my mother in long rambling letters. It's how I rationalized the move to her.

January 10, 1986
Dear Mammou,
I don't think I've been a very good husband these days with so much going on around me and so many factors to consider in deciding on moving. I remembered our sudden move from Rome and how you put family above career then. Kathryn and I got it all sorted out, I think, and we're definitely moving to Toronto. I hope it will give us some stability and a better feeling of having a home someplace in this mixed-up world. With all the problems in the Middle East, I feel that Canada is the safest place to be. Europe is too close to the strife and in an uproar, and I fear other terrorist attacks. The US may be the next target, so Canada is still the safest place for my growing family unless there's a world war. If this were to happen, we are all goners, anyway. So much for my political opinions and dire predictions! I have missed your teaching, and I'm looking forward to studying again with both of you. What truly counts for me now is not to be the next superstar, but to sing well and do justice to my art. On a happier note, even as I am making plans to move, I have also rented a villa in Aix-en-Provence for the summer, and you and Dad are invited to vacation with us.

My mother didn't like writing long letters like I did, so more often than not, she'd respond with a phone call, and we spoke for hours until I reminded her of the long-distance charges. She was ecstatic about our decision to move close to our families and promised to come to vacation in Aix-en-Provence with us.

Besides the decision about where to live, I was also preoccupied with the direction my career should take. The The Royal Opera House offered me the possibility to sing in the grand Verdi opera *Don Carlos* in March of the following year. I was insecure about tackling the role.

February 21, 1986
Dear Mammou,
It is now early morning, and I am sitting by the living room window listening to some Wagner—the Overture from the Flying Dutchman. The orchestration is magnificent, but somehow, it loses its beauty when the singers join in. Too bad Wagner never attempted to write an Italian opera. A mixture of Wagner and Verdi would have made an incredible combination.

The music helps me to collect my thoughts and put things in perspective. I have so many important decisions to make with the new baby coming and the move. Not sure if I'm coming to a dead end with myself and feel rather useless. I feel as if I'm good at what I do, but am I good enough to tackle more? I have a nice voice, good but not great like Dad's. I look good on stage but is it enough to compensate for the rest? The big success I had with the *Barber* here has given me back some confidence, but I cancelled the upcoming film of *Guglielmo in Vienna* and refused a recording with Placido Domingo. Why? In Vienna, they wanted me to sing with only four days of rehearsal, and with Domingo, they offered me Herman, a very small part, I thought. Now the Royal Opera House has offered me *Don Carlos* for next year, and I'm debating whether to take it or not.

I'd be right on schedule to what Dad had suggested three years ago, and I desperately need a new challenge to inspire me, yet I fear the heavy role of the Marquis de Posa might still be too early for me. Posa is the only Verdian role I would dare to attempt at this point. *Rigoletto* is still unimaginable and unattainable, and Father owns that role. I would have to give up a year or two of performing to study with him. What do you think?

Don Gino

She answered in a letter this time.

Dear Don,

Good for you for refusing Vienna and Domingo. Up to now, every time you have declined something that did not feel right for you, something better has come up, like *Don Carlos*, now. You're ready for Posa, but stop measuring yourself against your father. You're two very different singers. No doubt he was a great Posa in Paris, but you were seven years old when you first saw him in that role, and everything seems bigger and unattainable through the eyes of a child. Rather than try to emulate him, think of what you can do differently for that role from what he did. Make it your own. There are things you do on stage he cannot do anymore. By the way, do you know how much weight he has gained since we moved to Toronto? His knee operation was not very successful, and he's still suffering from pain. His extra weight doesn't help, but he won't stop eating, especially after each performance, and won't do his exercises. I'm also worried for his heart. I even suggested he get an exercise bicycle, but he laughed at the thought of riding a stationary bike that doesn't go anywhere. If you take the Posa role, I'll come to Paris for your final coaching.

I even discussed techniques with my mother in my long letters.

March 10, 1986
Dear Mammou,
Remember how the muscle just under my chin never worked properly? Now it's working very well. How did I discover this? Well, as I watched birds sing in a cage one day, I noticed a swelling under their beaks as they sang. It amazed me how the birds, though so tiny, can project a piercing sound audible from far—the right sound for an opera singer, not large but projected. So I tried to focus on the muscle under my chin until I felt a tiny swelling, and the sound became more projected. I also discovered this makes it easier to sing a low note and pop up to the high note without effort. Nevertheless, breathing is still a major issue, and I'm still

working hard on the positioning of the larynx. I miss my two teachers terribly.

For Easter of that year, she sent me a card with a scene of apple blossom trees with birds perched on the tree branches with a note.

Interesting observation about the birdies. The only problem is that birds always sing on one vowel, but you opera singers have five, A-E-I-O-U, not to mention that you can't sing your hearts out sitting on a branch. You must move. But if the technique works for you, sing like a swallow! Can't wait to see Rico and spend time with you in Aix-de-Provence this summer.

I spent the summer of 1986 in Aix-en-Province for two performances, *Don Pasquale* and *Don Giovanni*, which garnered me the nickname "The Don" in my family. Before leaving for *Don Pasquale*, I had the privilege of meeting Prince Charles and Princess Diana for a private concert and dinner hosted by the Honourable R. Roy McMurtry at the High Commission of Canada on Trafalgar Square in London. The Prince and Princess were both very open and gracious. I sat across from Princess Diana at the dinner table, and I even had the honour of dancing with her later that evening. After meeting them up close, I felt the utmost respect for them both. It must not be easy, I thought, being a Prince and Princess, carrying great responsibilities, and with very little freedom to be themselves. They were both very impressed by my performance and thanked me several times for a wonderful experience. My father would be singing for them at Expo '86 in Vancouver later in the year. Princess Diana asked me if I had a message for him. I jokingly told her to tell him that she thought the son was the better singer. With a mischievous smile, she said that she'd bring him my regards from London and would tell him that I was a marvelous son with an incredible voice.

In my first *Don Giovanni* in Aix-de-Province, in June, the critic for *Le Journal du Dimanche* wrote: « *Gino Quilico, acclamé à juste titre par un public sensible, a amplifié la justesse du ton et la longue sensualité d'un Don Giovanni, peut-être plus irresponsable que volontairement cynique et provocateur, mais qu'importe… .* » / "Gino Quilico, rightly acclaimed by a sensitive audience, amplified the accuracy of the tone and the long sensuality of a Don Giovanni, perhaps more irresponsible than deliberately cynical and provocative, but what does it matter…"

I had my revenge for the bad review I had received there the year before when I had sung the title role in *Orfeo*. I got booed there for the very first time. It had nothing to do with my singing but instead because the Maestro had changed certain traditions in the Baroque style music, and the purists did not like it. After opening night, with lots of bravos from the audience, *Le Figaro* gave me a raving review while *Le Monde* nitpicked on the orchestra, the music, and my style of singing Baroque. At the second night performance, I got booed from the upper left side of the stage. Only a few boos, but they went straight to my heart. It was very painful to me and discouraging. Maestro Corboz, the specialist in this kind of music, immediately came to me and expressed that I should ignore this small crowd of purists.

He had chosen me for the production and later a recording and feature film of the same opera, because he wanted a young and modern voice. He also used modern instruments in the orchestra, breaking with traditions since certain instruments from the past, such as trumpets, harps, etc., are very difficult to keep in tune. In the Baroque tradition, they tend to use more white voices, with very little tremolo. My voice is considered modern with a tremolo and hence the displeasure of the purists.

"Welcome to the world of stardom. You can now consider yourself a star after being booed at Aix-en-Provence," the Maestro told me. "One day, none of this nonsense will be important." He was right. Today, many modern voices like mine sing the Baroque repertoire, though some purists still do not like it. The French purists are the most unabashed with their boos, as I had also experienced when singing *Die Fledermaus* in 1983.

Though it's a world-renowned festival, the conditions backstage in Aix-en-Provence were a disorganized mess, with costumes and sets arriving at the very last minute and sopranos showing up without having rehearsed. However, after my second season performing *Don Giovanni* in the south of France, I didn't let any of these minor irritations upset me. I enjoyed the sun and ambiance and gave it my all.

Both Kathryn and I had felt most joyful while visiting the French countryside. I wanted to recreate the feeling, and that summer, I rented a nine-bedroom villa with an Olympic-sized swimming pool. I spared no expense, throwing many parties for my close friends and several international personalities. The list included my good friend Victor Melnikoff and his ballerina wife Nathalie Grosshenny, Diana Mulgan, Erick and Clarissa Hood, both psychiatrists, a ballerina from Geneva, Lea Havas, my British agents, my parents, and a very pregnant Kathryn. The stellar restaurant, Le Village, run by my friend, Jacki Attali, supplied all the gourmet food and drinks flowed for everyone.

Of that sun-filled summer, I wrote in my journal: "I feel as though this is a dream. How could it happen to me? I am here, and I am the star." I felt a sense of freedom as a free agent not bound by a house contract anymore and with authority to make my own decisions. My career was the strongest it had ever been—in retrospect, a magic period professionally. I had to refuse engagements for lack of time. Father's career was also at its peak, though he had closed the door to Europe and performed mainly in New York City at the Met. I felt optimistic I had made the right choice to move to North America.

I made a pact with Kathryn that if I were to sing all year round, including summer festivals in Europe, we should spend all my summer earnings to create our own unforgettable private festivals. We'd bring the children and a nanny with us for carefree family summer holidays. My parents and Kathryn then left for Toronto while I returned to Paris to tie up some loose ends. Before leaving, I gave away a Vespa that I had bought to one of the backstage crew. Riding it in Aix-de-Province had given me the same sense of freedom I had felt when riding my Solex in Rome as a young boy.

I joined Kathryn in Toronto a month later, when our daughter was born in August of 1986. This time Kathryn had her revenge and chose the baby's name—Sofia for wisdom—a name that suits our daughter well.

The family had moved to Toronto, but my career was still very much in Europe, and the Concorde became my plane of choice.

Chapter 30
Father and Son at the Met

We stayed in Toronto for one year, then moved permanently to Montreal and bought a Victorian-detached house in Westmount that had 10-foot ceilings, beautiful woodwork, stained-glass windows, and a nice-sized garden. That same year we also bought a house in Florida where we entertained family and friends.

Several reasons dictated the choice of moving to Montreal. I liked its cosmopolitan and European feel, its French character, and the fact we could have privacy away from our respective families and yet be close enough to visit. I also wanted my children to be fluent in French. Logistically, for my travel needs, it also made more sense. The international airport was a short drive away from our home in the centre of town. When living in Europe, I flew back and forth on the Concorde to cut down on travelling time only to drive hours to and from an airport in the far outskirts of Paris and London.

Having been a nomad for most of my life, I often had difficulty answering questions about my nationality. I was born in the US to parents of Italian origin who were themselves born in Quebec. As a young man, I lived in Canada, where I was exposed to both English and French cultures, especially in Montreal, where French is the predominant language. I had had homes in England and France before moving again to Canada in 1986. I carried both an American and Canadian passport.

I never questioned why, but up until November 1987, I had never thought of myself as a Canadian. An exceptional performance at the Met would change my identity crisis forever.

My Father and I made musical history at the Metropolitan Opera House! In a much-touted performance, we became the first father and son duo to perform together in the same opera in its 103-year existence. *The New York Times* had covered my debut at the Met one month earlier in Massenet's *Manon* with the headline, "Gino Quilico: A baritone's son makes Met debut." My father was a highly respected permanent singer at the Met, so it was not unusual that the media would highlight my relationship with him. With the announcement of the duo performance, the media gave us an even bigger build-up. I would sing as Lescaut, and Dad would perform the role of Count des Grieux. It was a small part for my father, and he only accepted the role to make the historical performance.

The TV cameras came to my parents' apartment in New York and filmed us as we played Mario Brothers video games together. "Sometimes the son brings out the boy in the dad," the announcer declared, and as we practised and discussed our roles, he added, "What a team, the Quilicos, what a package, note for note, the most dynamic family in opera to arrange an aria!"

The afternoon before the performance, I received a commemorative plaque and a private letter of congratulations from the then Prime Minister of Canada, Brian Mulroney:

Dear Mr. Quilico,
On Behalf of the Government of Canada, I am pleased to convey to you my warmest greetings and best wishes on this historical first performance by a father and son at the Metropolitan Opera House. Canadians and indeed, all those who have an appreciation of opera may take great pride in your accomplishments as well as your contribution to music in Canada and throughout the world. I know that your performance will reflect your commitment to musical perfection, and I trust that those in the audience this evening will be highly entertained.

Could the expectations be any higher?

Family members had flown to New York from Montreal for the momentous occasion. The cameras followed us as we prepared to go on stage. We knew there were many dignitaries in the audience, including the Canadian Ambassador to the US. It all added to the hype.

All the attention made both of us very nervous. I had never seen my father as jumpy before a performance as that evening. Watching him pace up and down backstage, a tense look on his face, for a while, I thought he might not be able to go on. Members of the orchestra with whom he had worked for years came to congratulate us, making him very emotional. They knew him well and understood what the evening meant for him. I may have hidden my anxiety better than him, but I was just as nervous inside.

Once on stage, the music and our respective roles took over, and we both sang as well as we ever did. "They needn't have given it a care," the reporter announced the day after, "as a package they brought down the house."

The audience honoured us with a standing ovation. The leading soprano, Carol Vaness, who sang the title role of Manon, graciously let us have the last bow as flowers showered upon us from the audience. We had experienced the same excitement emanating from the public when we had performed as a family in Montreal back in 1984. The music lovers in my parents' hometown had resoundingly welcomed them back. To be so honoured and acknowledged at the Met meant that we had both achieved the apex of our success. When a bouquet landed on my feet with a Canadian flag wrapped around it, I must confess I had a big lump in my throat. I saw it as a sign: at that moment, I felt truly Canadian for the very first time.

We had two dressing rooms be-decked with flowers, and I took every bouquet back to our apartment. My mother was radiant when she hugged us together and said, "I'm so proud of both of you!" I understood that this was more than just a successful performance. It was validation for the three of us of all that we had achieved separately and jointly as a family, and of our unique contribution to the larger opera family. For me, it became especially significant. I found my identity on stage singing next to my father! From then on, I've always given my identity as Canadian.

The General Director of the Metropolitan Opera, Mr. Crawford, gave us a private reception and surprised us by asking us if we'd be happy to sing again together in *The Barber of Seville* the following season. We had other joint performances. Some people questioned why my father would accept so many new and different roles from his repertoire, such as the Count des Grieux in *Manon* at the Met; later Bartolo in *The Barber of Seville*, and Leporello in *Don Giovanni* with the Canadian Opera Company and at the Met. My father did it because he was proud and excited to sing next to me, and we had lots of fun doing it. We were both two big kids at heart. And we never stopped playing with miniature toy trains as we had done at the old bicycle store whenever we had the chance.

We understood and respected each other's vocal qualities and differences. Even the critics never tried to compare us. I would never try to embrace my father's repertoire. Though I strove to sing more Verdi, the only role I would never sing was Rigoletto. That belonged to my father.

Chapter 31
Gino and Friends

Stability is not part of an opera singer's life. We move around to wherever opera companies produce the few right roles for our voices and repertoire. When I took on a role, I'd be away for a month and a half to two months at a time; a month and a half in Lyon, another stay in Seville, and then I'd be gone to prepare for another role in Hamburg, and so on. I had based my career in Europe, and so I was away from home ten months of the year. Home for me was a hotel room. My parents had always travelled together, bringing the family with them to Europe, and it was only for short separations that they left us with Nanni, my grandmother. When they settled in Toronto, the Met was only an hour away, and my father flew back and forth between performances. As a couple, my parents were never really separated for extended periods as Kathryn and I were. Singing in Europe and living in North America posed separation problems, especially since Kathryn and I had made a conscious decision not to disrupt the children's living patterns. During the school year, they stayed at home with Kathryn. I made sure that during all school breaks, the family would be together. Every summer, I rented a house and moved the children wherever I was performing. I hired a nanny to travel with Kathryn and engaged tutors for the children. At the time, money was no object, and I spent a fortune renting lovely vacation homes and hiring nannies. Thousand-dollar phone bills for long-distance calls were the norm. We had no Skype or WhatsApp at the time. I never fussed about money; Kathryn handled our finances. My preoccupation always centred around the welfare of the family and my all-consuming career. Still, with all this effort, it was difficult coming home for a week or two after being away for two months and playing father to the kids, trying to pick up where we had left off, keeping up with their stories at school, disciplining them for misbehaviour that had occurred weeks earlier. The distance took its toll on my marriage to Kathryn.

"You became famous too quickly," Kathryn would often tell me, or, "Stop playing the superstar." I must confess that I was not thrilled to perform the more banal house-husband duties such as taking out the trash or fixing leaky faucets after having lived big dreams and high emotions on stage and being treated like a celebrity by thousands of spectators. It was especially tough for me, shrugging off the persona of the roles I had taken on in the previous months or while mentally preparing to enter the next one. But meanwhile, Kathryn had to fill the role of mother and father to the children ten months of the year. We grew apart and communicated less and less. There were no angry screaming matches between us, but even when we were together in the same house, we were as distant as if we were miles apart. Kathryn sought professional guidance and urged me to do the same. I made a feeble attempt to attend a few meetings, but again, I had an international opera career and had very little time between performances. In hindsight, I must have known that joining my two worlds would be an impossibility. Despite my small hope, the void kept getting bigger and bigger.

I confided in my mother through long telephone conversations. Every time, she implored me to try harder. In a letter, she wrote,

> The foundation of your relationship is too strong. Don't forget that Kathryn has been through many hard times with you and has always been a great support to you, and is raising two wonderful children almost by herself. You have both invested too much in this marriage, and Rico and Sofia are the proof of that. Think of what brought you together, of what you each loved about each other rather than the negative forces that are interfering and trying to break you apart. You both must try harder.

I was troubled by our small spats and long silences, but with encouragement from my mother, I held onto the hope that once I became more secure in my career, I would have more time for the family. We would find our way.

My career continued to climb, particularly in film. In 1986, I finally made it to Cinecittà to play the title role in Monteverdi's baroque opera *Orfeo*. We filmed in the studio where many great films were made, from the spaghetti Westerns I favoured to *La Strada,* directed by Federico Fellini with Giuletta Masina and Anthony Quinn. Little did I know that in the studio next to ours was the man himself, Fellini, filming *Ginger & Fred* with Marcello Mastroianni and Giuletta Masina. We had the unexpected bonus and expertise of cameraman Giuseppe Rotunno, who had made many films with Fellini. One day as I exited the studio, I found myself in front of Marcello Mastroianni with his Borsalino hat, talking to Giuseppe, and I joined them. As we started chatting, a rather husky white-bearded man with an authoritative speaking voice joined in. I had no clue who he was, so when he left with Marcello, I asked, "Who is this man?" Surprised by my question, Giuseppe replied, "That's Fellini!" "Oh my gosh!" He had been my film idol. I regret not having taken a picture with this legendary man, but Marcello and I crossed paths several times in the studio cantina, and we took a picture together. My film, directed by Swiss Film director Claude Goretta opened at the Venice Film Festival.

Another memorable encounter happened in 1987 for a performance of *Carmen* at the London Royal Opera House conducted by Zubin Mehta. Playing Escamillo, as I was knocked down, I lost a note. Quickly, as I got up, I improvised a "la, la, la," to cover up the slip. From the corner of my eye, I looked at the Maestro and he smiled at me, knowing full well what had happened. I could have fooled the audience, but never Maestro Mehta. Later, in 2003, at a performance in Munich of *Les Troyes,* with Maestro Mehta, I learned that we shared the same April 29 birthday.

In the summer of 1988, I returned to film *La Bohème* in Cinecittà with Barbara Hendricks and José Carreras, directed by Luigi Commencini. It was a French/Italian co-production, and we had already filmed parts of it in Paris. The filming in Paris was particularly strange. We began the shoot during the summer, where they converted an outdoor courtyard into a wintertime scene. Fluffy balls of white cotton passed for snow on the edges of windows, and a truckload of salt had been spread to whiten the ground. The salt burned our eyes after a while, and we seemed to be constantly crying. We all carried hankies.

José and I shared the same trailer for our dressing room, and I began to notice that he always seemed very tired. We started by filming Act 3. We had recorded the singing in advance, and we lip-synched for the movie. Jose managed to finish a part of the third act but collapsed during a scene that brought the entire production to a halt. The last words he sang were, "*Addio senza rancor/*goodbye without rancour." The irony of these words only became evident as we all waited to know what was wrong with José. Finally, after a few days, the director announced that Jose was very ill with cancer and could not continue. They later reported that he suffered from acute lymphoblastic leukemia and was given a one in ten chance of survival. His final lyrics took on an even greater significance.

It all felt surreal, as if we were living our own tragic opera within an opera. It saddened me so much to hear that José was fighting for his life, especially as I had shared the same space with him and had experienced his gentle and kind ways as well as his great talent as a tenor. I had heard that his mother had died from cancer when he was eighteen years old and that her death had affected him greatly. Later, in his video biography, *José Carreras: A Life Story*, he stated, "Even now, every time I go on stage, I always, always, have a quick thought for her."

The director had to find another actor and restart the filming quickly, each day costing him a great amount of money to keep everybody in action mode. Many actors auditioned, but it seemed impossible to find a replacement who could learn the opera's lyrics in such a short time and lip-sync the music and imitate the voice of José Carreras. They found a young talented singer who already knew the opera by heart, who negotiated a solo recording to promote his real beautiful voice in exchange for lip-synching in the film. Luca Canonicci was selected, production resumed, and the rest is history. The film opened at a cinema on the Champs Elysée. I felt a great affinity for Carreras. I didn't need the salt to make me cry real tears at the opera's ending.

The happier ending in José's story is that he was in good medical hands, and he recovered. He underwent grueling treatment involving chemotherapy, radiation, as well as a bone marrow transplant. After his ordeal, he devoted much of his time to humanitarian work. He established the José Carreras International Leukemia Foundation to repay the debt he owed to medical science and improve other leukemia survivors' lives and care.

An interesting note is that the idea for the popular Three Tenors concerts, which started in 1990 in the Baths of Caracalla, in Rome, was conceived both as a fundraiser for his foundation and as a way for the other two great tenors, Pavarotti and Domingo, to welcome José, whom they considered their "little brother," back to the stage. It demonstrates that even the famous can have big hearts. In the process of that historic concert, they also managed to make opera and classical music accessible to millions of people worldwide.

I also made a small contribution towards helping others. In 1990, I was made Goodwill Ambassador to the United Nations High Commissioner for Refugees. At its beginnings, the program's mission was to promote the plight of refugees. Being a Goodwill Ambassador for the UNHCR is a more impressive role today than it was back then, even though Audrey Hepburn and my friend Barbara Hendricks had been ambassadors as well. I was a part of this organization for a year. I had my mother as a role model. I felt a duty to use my talent to help those in great need, as she had done for the *Water for Africa* project. I organized a fund-raising concert at Roy Thomson Hall in Toronto with the help of Barbara Hendricks.

Barbara and I had become good friends by then. We had met for the first time at the Paris Opera in the production of Gounod's *Romeo and Juliet*. Together we also sang in *Le Roi Malgré Lui, L'Elisir d'Amore, Don Pasquale*, and many other concerts, and of course, we shared the experience of filming the eventful *La Bohème* in Paris and Rome. Her children, Sebastian and Jenny, the same ages as mine, became friends with my children, and Barbara's husband, Martin Engstoem, was also my agent. Barbara has been a tremendous friend and has been there for me as I have been there for her. We both have the utmost respect for each other and our art form. The concert raised much-needed money for our cause.

I also did several interviews to bring awareness to a worldwide emergency that has become more acute with the years, but I never had the chance to go to the refugee camps. I was discouraged by the organizers to travel to remote locations for reasons of safety. I now regret not having gone to the camps personally.

That year, 1990, was as intense as ever, with performances in Europe and two new recordings, *Don Pasquale* and *Oedepe*. For every new role, I flew my mother in to coach me. We were both very excited for my upcoming performance of *La Bohème* in San Francisco with Luciano

Pavarotti, but my first interaction with the tenor turned out to be problematic and even confrontational.

We had all signed contracts for the specific dates of the rehearsals. I made sure that the dates did not interfere with my performance of Enrico in *Lucia di Lammermoor* at the Met. Then, at the last minute, they changed both the opera opening date and the rehearsal schedule at Pavarotti's request. Out of respect, I flew in for the first two days of rehearsal but then had to leave for New York to continue my shows. Luciano had not been aware of this conflict with my schedule, but he refused to continue rehearsing without the assigned baritone there. The San Francisco Opera Company put pressure on me to cancel my last two performances at the Met, or failing that, they would replace me with compensation. I was furious with Luciano for having put me in a very awkward position, first by changing his mind on the opening date and rehearsal schedules and then for not wanting to rehearse with my understudy. Still, I swallowed my pride and begged the Met to replace me with my understudy for the last two performances. They agreed, but, on principle, I felt it unfair losing compensation for the missed performances at the Met, through no fault of my own. When I brought this up with the management in San Francisco, they told me to take the next flight and did not hesitate to pay me for my two lost performances.

On my arrival in San Francisco, I was still quite annoyed by Luciano's divo demands, and so I decided to defiantly sing in full voice at my first rehearsal. I took Luciano by surprise, and I saw him do a 180 when he heard the skinny baritone with the big voice, but he gave me a nod and his mischievous smile of approval as if he understood my feelings. We became good friends from that moment on. In the end, I understood that he had not acted on a caprice but out of a commitment to giving the best performance possible by rehearsing with the appointed singers. He generously gave interviews to journalists from the CBC who had come to interview me in San Francisco, and he said the most flattering words about me on public TV. He invited me to New York on Pavarotti day, and spoke with his publicist Herbert Breslin to take me on.

Luciano also gave me many words of advice about life and career. Once he saw me pacing backstage with a long face, and he asked me what the matter was. I had just spoken to Kathryn on the phone and was worried about the fragility of our marriage. He took me aside and, in no uncertain terms, told me, "Never but never bring your personal problems to the theatre, and never let anyone see you with that face around here again!" Despite the fact that his own marriage of thirty-nine years to his first wife, Adua, was on the rocks, he never displayed any sign of distress on stage or backstage. I took his advice to heart, and I revelled in his company.

One evening we cooked pasta together at his New York condo where he and Kathleen Battle, the American lyric and coloratura soprano, sang Happy Birthday to me.

Luciano and I sang together in *L'Elisir d'Amore*, at the Met, and in Tokyo. We crossed paths many times at the Met while singing in different productions. On a TV show about the Quilicos, I was so pleased to hear a quote by Luciano, who singled me out and said these words: "Gino is a great talent, a great voice, a real personality, and a beautiful actor. He will be a Verdian baritone who will probably achieve one of the greatest careers of all time. He has everything. Audiences are wild about him. It's a great pleasure for me to see that."

On another occasion, on a video, he said, "It's a dream to sing with Gino, so strong so young, so incredible."

This spell of good fortune broke in 1991, while I was preparing for my debut at La Scala. My mother announced that she was ill and could not be there with me. I was in shock when she mentioned the word cancer. She had never complained of any illness or discomfort, though I learned later that she been diagnosed with cancer of the liver and had kept the doctor's prognosis hidden from me for many months. I left for Milano with threatening metaphorical dark clouds hanging over me. When we started rehearsals, I could not help but think of José Carreras, his ordeal, and his mother's death of the same illness. He survived, and I prayed every day that my mother would beat the odds despite her grave diagnosis. I called her every day, and I didn't want to burden her with the conflict that had developed between Maestro Gavazzeni and me, so I made up some stories to keep her happy.

Chapter 32
Drama at La Scala

The conductor Gianandrea Gavazzeni was as much a fixture at La Scala as the marble bust of Verdi in the foyer. For close to fifty years,.he had conducted the most important Italian opera singers, from Tito Gobbi to Franco Corelli and Renata Tebaldi to La Divina Maria Callas, and many more. He was also a respected composer, music critic, and writer with strong personal views on opera and musical interpretation.

When I walked onstage a few minutes late for our first rehearsal, he gave me a terse once-over without so much as a good morning or a nod of acknowledgment. I immediately sensed his disapproval. When I tried to joke about being late, he threatened to throw me out if I didn't respect rehearsal start-times, an exaggerated reaction I thought, as I had just flown in from Paris that same morning. I apologized with an extravagant bow, and before I could explain, he cut me off.

"There's no place for American stars at La Scala," he snapped. I wanted to respond that I was, in fact, a Canadian baritone but I held my tongue and just took my place. My mother had told me that the Maestro disapproved of opera recordings. He had been quoted as saying that "Music had to be seen as well as heard," and I concluded that he considered me a philistine and a lightweight because of my many recordings and my popularity.

I had sung with many egocentric directors before and had learned to manage their idiosyncrasies, but he turned out to be more of an ass than any of the others. Never before had I felt so personally targeted as I did by Gavazzeni's continuous disparaging comments; they made rehearsals irritating at first, then infuriating, and they weren't about artistic differences but rather petty criticisms and sarcasm. While he would simply ask someone else to restart a phrase, to express more or less emphasis, with me, he would invariably add some mocking commentary, such as "Where do you think you are? Singing in a bar?" or "Do you need a microphone? This is La Scala, not Radio City Music Hall!" He rarely addressed me by my name but as *l'Americano* and with a look and tone of voice as if that term itself explained his scorn. I had seen it happen before, directors taking out personal frustrations on secondary role singers or vulnerable ones in their first performances because they were less likely to react badly or walk out. The maestro's behaviour towards me made me feel targeted as such.

It took me a few days to notice that he directed his most acerbic remarks my way when I sang next to Denia Mazzoni, who played Musetta, my love interest. She was also Gavazzeni's wife. He was an eighty-two-year-old man married to the beautiful soprano, one-third his age. His insecurity got the best of him. I just happened to be, through no fault of my own, the sucker that sparked those insecurities. As I had always done, I played Marcello's role as a ladies' man with verve and great enthusiasm, including the love scenes with Musetta. Those particular love scenes did not go over well with the Maestro, and I seemed to be getting under his skin. Denia herself took me aside once and told me not to take his harsh words to heart. I didn't want to make my private pain public, but I had learned just before arriving that my mother had a few months to live if her experimental therapy didn't work. Under the mental strain, I snapped and started referring to him as Maestro *Rompiscatole* outside the theatre for busting my chops. Mirella Freni, a superb soprano, also sensed my tension and gave me advice about the director, "*Non ne vale la pena,*" she told me. In other words, it was not worth getting upset over him. Both singers must have observed this behaviour before.

. Singing at the legendary La Scala had meant more to me than almost any other regular performance. It meant going back into the history of opera and becoming part of that legendary history, not only for my sake but for that of my family. That I had to experience it with this irrationally jealous man who took his insecurities out on me enraged me, especially since I was suffering inside and needed consoling myself. Then as we got closer to the opening, I was feeling feverish and chilled. I went to bed early each night, afraid I might get sick with a cold—the worst possible condition before a performance. I told my mother I was faking a sore throat to get back at the Maestro because I didn't want to worry her. One night, I could not fall asleep, and when I finally did, I had the weirdest of dreams .

> *I dreamed I am on stage performing, but suddenly, I find myself running backstage while an aging maestro pursues me with his baton. I look back and see a woman and my old nemesis, the dorky bass who had walked off with my first wife, also running after me. Why are they pursuing me, I think, when I was the jilted lover? But I never actually scuffle it out with anyone. I elude them, looking for hiding places while the maestro is never far behind me, following me through the dark corridors of the opera house. As in many recurrent dreams, my feet and legs are made of lead, and I'm stuck on the same spot, terrorized by the impending danger and not able to find my way back to the stage for the second act. I panic.*

In the morning, I didn't wake up relieved at the realization that it had only been a nightmare. Feeling physically sick, with pent-up feelings of fear about my mother's illness and anger at the conductor, I carried the sense of dread with me throughout the following days. It was as if some destructive force continued to follow me at the most crucial of times and contrived to take away all that I had achieved. Whenever the director raised his hands with the baton and looked at me with stern eyes, I felt threatened and wanted to run away. It was a panic that had accumulated over the years but that I had kept in check and hidden from colleagues. It dredged up old insecurities and imaginary terrors during the rehearsal of an all-important debut. I was afraid I would not be able to give my very best and fabricated stories of petty arguments with the conductor to prepare my mother if I became mentally and physically incapacitated and unable to perform.

I spent time before the opening at the Duomo Cathedral to ask God for strength and guidance. Then my father's appearance before the performance surprised me. He brought me a gold chain with a medallion of a wolf image—an Italian amulet of good luck. Both he and Mother wore one around their necks. She had wanted to give me one long before but could not find one outside Italy. "*In bocca al lupo,*" he said. His warm

160

embrace calmed me and gave me the courage I so badly needed to go on stage. The audience rewarded me with a standing ovation at curtain time. The Maestro didn't congratulate me, but he stopped harassing me for the rest of the run.

My father and some dear friends were in the audience to encourage me. I felt very lucky and grateful for their moral support. A friend from San Francisco, Maria Manetti, came to Milano just for my debut and threw a private party for me after the opening night at Biffi, the restaurant next to the theatre. The day after, whether from the strain, exhaustion, or nerves or because I had caught some nasty bug, I suffered a high fever and had to cancel the second night, but I recovered and did complete all the other scheduled performances.

Once back home, I became preoccupied with my mother's failing health, but with support from the rest of the family, I was able to focus on my commitments and rid myself of imaginary demons, if only for a while. I made time to be at my mother's side as much as I could. I took her to Florida for a month, and I bought a boat, a 30-foot Sea Ray weekender, to distract her from her pain and remind her of our carefree days on the beach in Ostia. I soon realized that though well-intentioned, boating was not the best activity for her. The rocking made her nauseous, and I had to bring her ashore after only a few minutes.

My mother was part of an experimental cancer study and had to be injected intravenously a few times each day to control the pain. Kathryn was the one who took care of this in Florida. In Canada, she shared the task with David. She would fly from Montreal to Toronto every Friday night with the children to relieve David and fly back home on Sunday night.

My father looked lost when he was with us, and he seemed not to know what to do with himself. Part of him was already missing. Yet on stage, he had to put on a happy face. I felt sad for him when he had to fly to New York for the City Opera production of *The Most Happy Fella* while dealing with my mother's cancer and suffering from knee pains. It's the ironic reality of a performer's life—to laugh as you suffer inside. When we were all together, I would force my mother to get up and accompany me at the piano hoping that the enjoyment derived from music would give her strength.

Then on September 21, 1991, surrounded by all of us, she was gone and left my father and me bereft and alone.

Chapter 33
The Show Must Go On

The day after my mother's funeral, I had to return to San Francisco to respect my contractual obligations and put on the face of free-loving Don Giovanni, whether I felt like him or not. More distracted than usual, I suffered my first onstage accident: I landed badly on my back and on both elbows for a scripted fall that I had acted many times before. It crushed my nerves and caused severe numbness in my fingers that has never really disappeared. But I continued the series of performances, like an automaton, despite physical and emotional pain.

But as life never stops, I made another of my many acquaintances during this Don Giovanni run that resulted in an unexpected friendship. After one of my performances, while I was getting out of costume and make-up with the help of my dresser, there was a light knock at my dressing room door. In came a smiling and vivacious woman with long curly hair. She congratulated me profusely on my performance. I had no clue who she was though her face looked familiar, and I knew that if they had allowed her to come backstage after the show, she must be some well-known personality. I thanked her, and she left. My dresser immediately exclaimed, "Didn't you recognize Joan Baez?"

"*The* Joan Baez? Shit!" I said. I knew of her, of course, as a folk singer with a reputation as an activist for peace but had never met her. I felt foolish for not recognizing her and upset that I had not taken the time to acknowledge her properly. "She must think I'm a real snob," I thought. After changing, I started down the stairs to exit the opera house, and there she was, crossing the hallway heading for the door.

I screamed out, "Joan Baez!" She stopped in her tracks, and I yelled, "Would you like to have a drink?" Surprised or maybe amused by my loud voice or invitation, she laughed and said, "Okay."

We headed out together and entered a hotel bar across the road. In the lobby, some servers came towards us and offered us a complimentary glass of champagne. We looked at each other, surprised by the gesture. I figured they had recognized her. We accepted graciously. After sipping the champagne, another person approached us and asked if we were part of some business conference. We shrugged our shoulders, and then they asked us to leave. Joan lifted her glass and said, "Bottoms up!" She downed the champagne and pitched the glass against the wall. After having personified wine-loving and crazy Don Giovanni all evening, I did the same with flair. And like two small misbehaving kids, we ran out of the bar and had a tremendous laugh. We called it a night, but the next day, which was my day off, Joan and her sister, picked me up at the hotel in real style—in a white stretch limousine. They took me all over San Francisco and the surrounding area. It was the beginning of a beautiful relationship. She came to Montreal as my guest a few months later on a visit with her son. I returned the favour and, with Kathryn, took them all around Montreal in my red convertible.

Soon after San Francisco, I flew to New York for the December 19 premiere of a new opera, *The Ghosts of Versailles*, with music by John Corigliano and directed by Colin Graham. It was much-anticipated since it had taken seven years longer to complete, well past its intended due date of 1983 to celebrate the Met's 100th anniversary. Corigliano and librettist William Hoffman adapted the opera from a 1792 French play, *La Mère Coupable* by Pierre Beaumarchais. It parodied and satirized the excesses of Marie Antoinette and her entourage.

I remembered how excited my mother had been when I took on the role to sing opposite Teresa Stratas, Hakan Hagegard, Renee Fleming, Graham Clark, and Marilyn Horne. The work was conceived as a grand *opera buffa* because Corigliano incorporated both elements of the grand opera style with a large chorus, extravagant costumes, dancers and special effects, and the silly antics of the *opera buffa*. My role of Figaro was comical and high-spirited, requiring much energy and dash on my part.

Coming barely three months after my mother's death, I went into the role wondering if I could perform it to my fullest ability. Reality set in that my mother was gone forever when I arrived in New York, and she was not there for rehearsals. She would have flown in to coach me for such an important and demanding role.

Still, I put all of my efforts into the performance, but after each final bow, I returned to my hotel room feeling as if someone else, my double, had gone through the motions of a Figaro and that I had then left that man in the costume room of the Met until the next performance. The other me walked through the New York streets brightly lit with Christmas decorations, painfully sad at the thought of my first Christmas without my mom and having to pretend cheerfulness while my heart was heavy with grief.

My father also suffered terribly at the loss of my mother. She had been at his side not only as a wife but as a precious collaborator. I accepted his depression as a normal part of the grieving process. I tried to make time for him whenever I could. I spent hours with him at his New York apartment when he was covering roles at the Met, set up a room for him at my home in Montreal where he stayed with us for long periods, and he visited my home in Florida where he loved to take my boat out beyond the reef. We spent time together in Japan while both of us were on tour in Asia. He was most definitely slowing down as he adjusted to life without Mom as well as coping with his recurrent knee problem. When I was away, Kathryn would check on him, and she helped him with all his legal papers, looked after his finances, scheduled his appointments, and, at his request, acted as his agent in Canada.

The rest of the family became perplexed when they noticed him in the presence of young women singers. I found it amusing and was not overly worried. My father gave the appearance of a fun-loving teddy bear, but I also knew his serious and logical-thinking side. He was no fool and was too wise to be hoodwinked by some career-climbing young singer. I was wrong.

Chapter 34
Disconnection

My father had been my teacher and my idol. I had never had any serious confrontations with him, except for the usual generational conflicts during my teen years. The situation changed and slowly started deteriorating a year or so after my mother's death, and often I felt that whatever I said to him was wrong and taken as criticism. When my father complained of feeling tired one day, I answered that he might be working too hard and that maybe he should slow down. He turned angrily at me and shouted back, "I'm not ready for the cemetery yet. Get a plot for yourself." I could no longer kid around with him as I had always done without him snapping back at me.

Concerned about my immediate family life and career, I may not have been as attentive to his changing moods until I saw him slowly sliding away from us, distancing himself from the family, wanting solitude, and not responding to my invitations. I could not understand the reason for the change of personality. Still, I kept my impressions to myself, hoping that time would heal his depressive state and that he would soon return to his loving self.

Then we heard that he had met a career pianist and teacher, twenty-three years his junior. They carried on a professional relationship for a while, but when it developed into a personal one, he kept it secret from us at first, maybe fearing that we would disapprove. The opposite was true. I was happy that he had found a companion and someone with a shared interest in music.

They married in 1993, two years after my mother's death. In the beginning, all was well for everyone. Seeing Dad come out of his depression after my mother's death made us all very happy. He found new comfort with his new pianist who worked hard at promoting Dad and her relationship with him. Some of the limelight created fell on her too. With the name Quilico attached to hers, her piano recitals became more and more in demand.

When I visited their new home and found it utterly devoid of any reminders of our family's history, I became eerily aware that Father had closed that part of his life. Although I had asked to have some of the photos and mementos that had been put in storage, other than the ones I had already taken, I was given none.

Because she didn't want to intrude of his privacy with his new wife, Kathryn handed over all the banking and financial papers that she had been looking after. I was devastated to hear from other family members that he felt wronged and unappreciated by Kathryn and me, and I wondered who had put those ideas in his head. I tried to make peace by organizing a family dinner in Toronto, then wrote him a letter explaining that his two grandchildren missed him, but no response came. I got the silent treatment.

My personal life was also suffering. While in Buenos Aires in 1993, rehearsing for *Don Giovanni*, my heart was heavy, and I had great difficulty putting on the act of brashness and enthusiasm that the role demands. Marriage counseling had not brought Kathryn and me any closer. I sensed her unhappiness when I was home, and I feared we were heading for a divorce. The thought paralyzed me. I had lost my mother, was slowly losing my father, and my marriage was rocky at best. I asked myself, why sing, and for whom, when my family was disintegrating, and the world I had known was coming to an end. I could no longer confide in my mother, but I pretended I could, and in the evenings, when alone in my hotel room, I wrote notes to myself as if writing letters to her.

There are times in life when we put ourselves into little corners and fear the world. I feel so little and helpless at times, and so alone! Will I be able to go on stage tomorrow evening and give my all? It's as if someone is sneaking behind me and, when least expected, zaps me and my energy. Confidence drops to the floor. What a Creep! I would love to kill him if I could!

I tried to remember my mother's words, "Focus on your own energy and the good within yourself. Stop the person who whispers negative thoughts in your ear that tells you that you cannot do it. He is the most destructive creature that lives in your mind."

I understood that like a germ that had entered my body, always there waiting for weak moments to penetrate and destroy, I had to battle him constantly and find ways to neutralize him by building up an army of positive thoughts. That I was able to write down my feelings and recognize the problem was a step forward, and I resolved to look for ways to stop the old self-destructive pattern and fight the despair that took hold of me more and more often.

In public, my father and I gave the appearance that all was like before, and we often still sang together. The opera world, especially in Canada, had not forgotten Lina Pizzolongo, and naturally, both my father and I spoke about mother and her contribution to our careers during interviews. After one such interview, I saw his new wife pull Father aside and speak to him angrily. Was it because we had spoken about mother and not her? I wondered. I saw him coming out of their conversation as a reproached child, drawn and white as a ghost, without defending himself, and I understood that he was afraid of displeasing and losing her. I came to see how great his loneliness was.

There were many troubling arguments between my father and me, always spurred on by complaints that I was not acknowledging his wife in public. "She has tried to erase Mother's memory," I reminded my father. "I can't even say her name, let alone praise her in public."

Thankfully, my career gave me the greatest satisfaction. In 1995, I received a Grammy Award for my participation in the recording of *Les Troyens*. The following year, I sang my first Verdian role in *Falstaff* at the Met. Singing Verdi signified a new milestone for me, something I had aimed for during much of my artistic career as a baritone. But I had no one there to share my achievement. It hurt me deeply that my father didn't come to the performance when I knew he was in New York at the time. After the show, I went for a drink at a bar across from the Met on Broadway and 64th Street, and I was surprised to see my father and his wife sitting there. They made some excuses for not attending the performance when in the past, he had happily crossed the globe to all my most important performances. I was crushed at their insensitivity and devasted that my father could be so oblivious to what was happening to his family ties.

I remembered how disconcerting it had felt to see all traces of Louis Quilico's history with Lina Pizzolongo and Gino Quilico removed from their home. What does she have to lose by admiring the family's past achievements? I had asked myself then. I later understood that his wife could only feel secure in her new position by erasing Lina Pizzolongo's memory. The erasure continued in the public sphere as well.

The realization that she tried to erase the narrative of my mother's contribution to my father's success was made clear to me when in 1995, at the Teatro Colon in Buenos Aires, a colleague referenced a book written by his wife as a conversation between her and my father. I had not read the book but was told that the author had asked Father to explain his first wife's role as his voice teacher, as had been reported in the past. They never even mentioned my mother by name. Shocking to me, he now responded something to the effect that his first wife's contribution had been overstated, some kind of myth, even though he had thanked her publicly many times for it. He stated that, finally, he needed to tell his story without feeling obliged toward the family.

I wanted to yell: "Dad, how can you have forgotten both Mother and the family? Was it not Mother that dared you to pursue a singing career, or she'd leave you? Was it an illusion when her parents sold their home in Montreal so you could afford one in New York to pursue your dream? What about when her mother played Nanni to us children for years so Mother could accompany you as you travelled around the globe for your concerts? Were the years and years of Mother playing piano for you and helping you rehearse your roles a myth too? I witnessed it! I remember sitting under the piano as a boy, listening to the two of you rehearsing the scores for hours, note by note!"

Oh Dad, no one, but no one, could dismiss the god-given gift of a voice without which you would never have made it as a great baritone, or the role of the great vocal coaches you had throughout your career, but to dismiss as a myth Mother's years of dedication and devotion to you and your voice, must have made her ache more than even the spirit she had become should endure!

To wipe out those years and the unity of our family that she had striven for with the stroke of the pen in one question must have made Mother suffer as much as it infuriated me. The reported following question in the same conversation broke my heart. Father completely dismissed his relationship with me by stating that because we're very different, we should each pursue our own separate careers

I was already well established in my career and no longer needed his help, but I still needed his companionship and love. Yes, my father and I were different, both in voice and in temperament. He was a true Verdian baritone; I a lighter lyric baritone more suited for French opera. Our physiques were also different. He was a heavier man who didn't like to exercise, while I took part in many sports, was more agile on my feet, and a better dancer on stage. Behind his boisterous voice and physique, my father hid many insecurities, mainly due to some missed educational opportunities as a young man. He had a library full of books that he never read. He never studied music, and that is why my mother's collaboration had been so precious to him, especially in the early years. Nonetheless, he had mastered his art through the strength of his character, intuition, wisdom—and always had integrity for whatever he pursued. A straight shooter, he never compromised his principles to appease the whims of particular directors. I learned a lot from him in this respect. We accepted each other's strengths and weaknesses. Our differences had never gotten in the way before or pulled us apart, the way this was suggested in that statement.

Those were words that had been put in my father's mouth. I could only cry out: "Dad, you were my teacher! I have been your protégé. What happened to the family package?"

There was no other mention of the work we had done together and of us as a family besides these two statements in the whole book, as if the life we had lived before had never existed.

As artists, we work hard at studying and entering our roles. Sometimes a personal situation coincides with a performance that punctuates that role and makes it more real than real. When I heard of those two quotes while in Buenos Aires, I was singing Valentin in *Faust*. Faust is an aging scholar who is deeply depressed and is considering suicide over his lost youth. An infernal figure, Mephistopheles, appears and offers to change his goblet of poison for an elixir of youth, but with a catch. Faust must promise to exchange his position on earth with that of Mephistopheles;

in other words, sell his soul. Faust disgraces Valentin's sister, Margaret, and Valentin, a soldier, is determined to avenge his sister's honour, even if he does so motivated by the social norms of the times and also blaming his sister. In impersonating the role of Valentin, I fought the power of evil with all the conviction that I could muster as I understood that as Faust sold his soul in exchange for his youth, my father had sold his family for the same elusive dream.

I stopped speaking to my father.

Chapter 35
Breakup

Things had gradually fallen apart for Kathryn and me. Outwardly, we went through the motions and kept the family together but there was little emotion. I could have continued to perform like an automaton, travelling from country to country, from city to city, from stage to stage, focusing on my recordings, my videos, my special performances, and seeing the family for short snatches of time. But Kathryn's unhappiness deepened.

We spent the end of 1996 in New York where I was appearing in *La Bohème*. As much as we tried to pretend to be cheerful, the warmth and excitement of spending New Year's celebrations together as husband and wife were clearly absent. Once back home, our silences and unhappiness grew palpable. She had gone to see a psychologist, and that allowed us to finally open a dialogue and acknowledge the chasm that we had allowed to form between us.

We had been married for seventeen years, and had long tried to solve our own conflicts, but now we were stuck. The idea of a trial separation took hold. When separation is discussed, not after vicious arguments, but after sharing wonderful moments and experiences, it is difficult not to ask yourself what could have been done to avert a breakup. It was a sad and painful dénouement.

We acknowledged the void caused by my travel and career, but that alone could not have been the culprit. Our different personalities and priorities had never quite fit together. Though we shared the love for our children and we both strove to offer them a good home life, our goals in life had been different from the very beginning. I was ambitious and craved grandeur in all facets of my existence, whereas Kathryn was more reserved and content with a quieter lifestyle. Obsessed by my rising international career, I tolerated and accepted the erratic pattern that such a schedule demanded while Kathryn found it unsustainable. Since birth, my parents had instilled in me the idea that nothing short of success would do. When I was born, both my parents were pursuing their dream despite day-to-day preoccupations and deprivations. I was in my mother's womb when my father won the Met audition that started his career. This pursuit was part of my DNA.

Separation was not considered because of another woman, as was the case for many men in my circle. I simply felt that our relationship as husband and wife was no longer tenable. I had strong feelings for Kathryn and wanted her happiness. We promised ourselves that whatever our decision, we would do our best to remain friends. My next trip would take me to Amsterdam for four months to sing in the production of *Eugene Onegin*, and we agreed after much reflection to tell the children before I left. Sofia, who was 12 at the time, was the most upset. She blamed both of us for not trying harder. I left with the awful feeling that I had somehow failed everyone in the family.

When I returned the following spring, we sought professional help again, but even the mediator did not see a possible outcome for our troubled marriage. My schedule was the thorn. I blamed neither Kathryn nor myself. We were both at fault for being unable to reconcile our different needs, but maybe those needs were not reconcilable. I could no more stop pursuing my career than Kathryn could live the frenzied life of the travelling entertainer I had become. I realized that even if I could have convinced Kathryn to continue, I doubted we would have made it in the end. It was painful to accept the end of a marriage that had been built on mutual love.

Our trial separation became official, but it remained a private matter. I did not want my personal pain in the news or gossip columns. With my next singing engagement, *L'Elixir D'Amour* in Marseilles, coming up, there was no time to find a proper place to live, so I moved into a temporary furnished apartment in Montreal. There was no dispute over the house in Westmount, which I left to Kathryn. I took only my trophies and music mementos. Only several months later did I return home long enough to find a place of my own, a one-bedroom studio apartment, not far from the family home. When I received people at my new apartment, I told them it was my studio. I kept the breakup secret from the media; there had never been much media interest in my private life, and that's the way I wanted it.

We only divorced ten years later, after Kathryn met and wanted to marry Peter Trent, then mayor of Westmount. Kathryn and I have remained good friends throughout and are still very supportive of each other.

In September of 1997, I sang at the Metropolitan Opera for the opening of *Carmen* in the presence of Bill and Hillary Clinton. When I met them after, I offered them a CD of my recording of *Le Secret* with Quebec pianist Alain Lefevre. That recording was especially meaningful for me as my mother's memory had inspired the performance. I remember her playing the melodies on the piano with my father singing.

Alain and I had recorded the CD in a studio near St. Adele in the Laurentians north of Montreal a few months after my separation. The studio faced a beautiful lake. On the first day of the recording, I was overcome with emotion and lost my voice. I was physically unable to sing. Everybody was kind to me and suggested I go down to the lake to relax. Feeling alone and overwhelmed, I asked my mother for help. I am a believer in spirits and their power. A gush of wind came from the lake, and with it I felt a boost of energy. I returned to the studio shortly after and did not stop recording for several days. Almost miraculously, some 99 % of that CD is a live recording, which means no editing or retakes. Very often, recordings are corrected by splicing in corrections between two takes, but this recording flowed perfectly, uninterrupted. I felt as though my mother had been beside me through the whole experience. When released, the CD received great acclaim. In France, they praised my French, while, oddly enough, in Quebec, they criticized it. Go figure! I was very proud of my work on this CD, which is why I offered it to the Clintons.

Later in December, I received a letter from Bill Clinton: "Dear Gino, Thank you so much for the copy of *Le Secret*. It brings back fond memories of seeing you at the Metropolitan Opera. Hillary and I appreciate you sharing your work with us, and we send you our best wishes."

Instead of rejoicing at the expression of appreciation by the Clintons, I remained sad that I could not share it with the people I had loved.

I wrote more and more letters to myself whenever I was away and alone.

Brussels, May 8ᵗʰ, 1998

Well, I have come around to realize that I have lost feeling. It seems that somehow I have placed feelings into sex—the only place that makes me feel alive. I have lost connection with my heart. I must come to terms with this and the many obstacles that have caused this closure from life. Starting as a child, I never had the chance to maintain close friendships, only temporary ones. The strong model images of my father and mother always made me feel the need to aim high to prove myself to them. My travels throughout the world, as far back as I can remember, have brought me many great pleasures but also cost me friendships and relationships. In my love life, I was betrayed once by a woman I trusted and believed and then failed terribly at my marriage with Kathryn, a pillar in my life and probably the last thing that kept me sane and together. I had believed that I had been fortunate in love with Kathryn as my wife, but the passion left us along the way. I accepted leaving her because I thought she deserved better than me. I've created a wall by closing my heart to protect myself. I must find a way to break down this barrier that has become too natural and too normal to me and, at times, even comfortable.

My energy goes up and down, with no longer extreme highs, but the lows hurt hard. Serious love relationships seem impossible, and self-confidence depends mainly on what I believe is people's perception of me. I seek approval from others and never look within myself. This has not always been the case. It's something that has crept up on me over the years, and I cannot blame one specific situation or time in my life that has brought me to this nowhere land. I try hard to understand. My recurrent feelings of distress follow thoughts of my mother's loss, my father's abandonment, and, finally, the end of my marriage. My children are the only stability in my life and probably the only reason I am still here. I live in fear that my voice will let me down because of the direct connection with my heart. I have never sung strictly on technique but rather with my soul. My schooling and the two mentors who taught me this truth are no longer around to support me. Now I feel as though people are constantly judging me and waiting for me to screw up. How terrifying!

My sexual relationships comfort me. They fill in the gaps, and I need them desperately. Is it wrong to enjoy the temporary intimacy that they provide, though I know that it is only an escape from reality? How long will they satisfy me?

Chapter 36
Nadia

In between bouts of depression, loneliness, and career ups and downs, I let my sexual drive take over for fear of losing it, as had happened after my first breakup. After the separation, I went on a rampage and made love with whoever came my way. Then I met Nadia, which is Aida backward without the last consonant. I saw her as the trophy in my triumphal march over my sense of dejection and loneliness. Instead, she turned my world topsy-turvy in the craziest roller-coaster ride I could have ever imagined.

An untamed goddess from the Comoro Islands, off the southeastern coast of Africa near Madagascar, I met her in Marseilles. She was thirty years younger than me, skin smooth as sculpted onyx, body lithe and nimble as an alley cat. She conquered me as much with her youth as with her beautiful blackness. I was smitten and fell genuinely in love.

But like a feral feline, Nadia soon displayed a split personality that bordered on schizophrenia—happy, sweet, and delicious at one moment, spiteful and hurtful in another. I was at the height of my career and could have enjoyed all the perks that come with success. I thought I could best enjoy them with Nadia and spend the rest of my years with her. My previous experience with my first wife, a troubled woman with anger issues, should have been a warning. Ours was a tormented relationship from the start.

I brought her to Montreal, and she accompanied me everywhere I went. I introduced her to my children and all my music friends. I encouraged her to return to school or learn some occupation so she wouldn't be bored while I rehearsed or travelled, but mood swings became more and more painful the longer we lived together. When she was sweet and desirable, I considered marrying her. But then we'd have the most horrific arguments, and I'd rack my brain trying to understand what had brought them on. For no apparent reason, she'd give me the silent treatment, which usually coincided with an important debut or opening night. At those moments, I relived my dark days with Anne-Marie all over again, and these were hellish. Worse still, when angry, she would turn violent. Once she threw a beer bottle at me, which landed on my eye and could have caused permanent damage. Another time, she scratched my face with her long nails leaving red marks on my face for weeks. When her toxic moods became unbearable, I'd send her back to Marseilles and see other women, vowing to never seek her again. She would cool off and call me, and I could not resist taking her back. It was like an addiction. We had a few good moments together until the cycle started again, and she tortured me with pain and rage.

The children noticed how beaten down I became when I was with her. Yet, I wanted no one else. I had no one to talk to when I felt anguished. The children were still young and could not understand. I was too embarrassed to discuss my feelings with Kathryn. My mother was not there, and my father had become a stranger. I roamed the world in perpetual anxiety enduring periods of high exhilaration and deep despair.

While on vacation with Nadia in Marseille in 2000, I received a call from Kathryn that my father had been in hospital for a knee injury and there had been serious complications. I took the first flight to Toronto, and while on the plane, I learned from the in-flight news that my father had died. I wanted to cry out in pain, but I was strapped down in a plane surrounded by strangers who would not have understood my tears. I closed my eyes, plugged my ears and turned on the music to drown my anger, but was still crushed by it.

I never had the chance to reconcile with my father. *Why did we stop talking?* I wondered. I didn't blame myself because I knew I had done all I could to save our relationship. Instead, I blamed him, at least until I faced the casket and felt my father's spirit enclosed within it. He'll never sing again, I thought. A rush of silent tears mixed with love towards the man whose voice was forever silenced, made me stretch my hand to touch the casket and connect with him. I whispered, *I forgive you.*

I was unable to speak at his funeral in Toronto but mustered all my strength to speak up at his second funeral in Montreal.

"I knew the man and the artist," I said, and those were profoundly felt words.

In the days following his death, I dug deep into my soul, and I understood Louis Quilico, the man, better than ever before. I had appreciated the artist much more than the man. I now understood what it must have felt like for him to be left alone, searching for love from a woman nearly thirty years younger, finding comfort with her, and having to give up all other relationships to be assured of that love. He had given me everything but had fucked up at the end. He lost control of his life in the last six years. I understood and I forgave him but felt more than ever the pain of loss and sense of disorientation as I anticipated that same fate for myself. I especially understood my own dependency on Nadia. After all, my father and I are not that different, I thought, but it would still take some time to wean myself from that dependency.

I rationalized my numerous infidelities to Nadia as vengeance for her erratic and destructive behaviour; and I kept excusing her actions as unresolved anger issues. Then she committed the one mistake that finally broke her spell over me—she tried to come between my children and me.

Nadia accompanied me to my daughter Sofia's high school graduation ceremony along with Kathryn and the rest of the family in Montreal. I was proud of Sofia and the beautiful and sensible young woman she had become. Unlike many young people her age, she appreciated the simpler, quieter things in life. She had studied well, and I knew that this day was important to her. After the ceremony, we were all invited to a restaurant to celebrate. I naturally wanted to go, but Nadia took me aside and said she was not comfortable attending. I tried to convince her, but she insisted. I was afraid of crossing her and causing a scene. In the end, I found an excuse for why we couldn't attend. I saw the look of disappointment on my daughter's face, but did nothing. I followed Nadia to the car.

While driving away, the realization that I had lied to my daughter hit me hard. I expressed my displeasure to Nadia. She flew into a rage and started kicking me while I drove, almost making me lose control of the wheel. *What have I become?* I thought to myself. *I've lied to my daughter to keep the peace with this troubled woman!*

I remembered my father's whitened face when his second wife chastened him for not mentioning her name at one of our interviews, and he didn't dare contradict her. Did he miss my *Falstaff* debut to please his new wife? Was it the fear of upsetting her that kept him from answering my invitation to come and see my children? His father had also distanced himself entirely from his family after he remarried a younger woman. I saw myself making the same errors that my father and my grandfather had committed before me. It had cost them their families. In a moment of clarity, I saw that I too was slowly cutting myself off from my children without noticing it. When we got home and safely distanced from the possibility of a car accident, I finally told Nadia that she had crossed a line. The day after, I looked for a rental apartment for her. I gave her a cheque for $20,000 and my car and told her to get out. She accepted and drove out of my life forever.

Chapter 37
Help From My Friends

Over the course of my career, I crossed paths with many egocentric and obnoxious personalities. But it was the beautiful creative souls who truly believed in and lived for the sanctity of their art, who became a source of inspiration. Some offered words of encouragement when I was down. Once, Barbara Hendricks gave me a book as a gift, *Living in the Light*, and spoke to me about "creative visualization", an important tool in singing. I often referred to the book when feeling despondent or having problems with vocal technique.

A few years later, while in New York, mezzo-soprano Denyse Graves had also given me a book that she thought would help me. Maybe both had sensed that I needed some guidance. At the time, I did not feel the necessity to read the book; its title, *Conversations with God,* intimidated me. I remembered my father talking about having spoken to God while in Russia. I didn't question him then, but neither did I fully grasp what he claimed to have experienced. Yet, I kept both books in my travel suitcase, just in case.

In the aftermath of my obsession with Nadia and feeling empty and alone, I searched for *Conversations with God*, leafed through the book, and it finally spoke to me. It led me to identify with the number three and how everything in life revolves around the trinity: Father, Son, Holy Ghost; morning, afternoon, night. I made my own trilogies: The beginning, the middle, the end of a story; birth, growth, death; the child, the boy, the man/artist. I thought of the relationships between these parts as well as the forces that can wreak havoc and disrupt the harmony that must flow from one part to the next. I understood that doubt and fear are part of a man's fulfilment from childhood and boyhood and that he cannot give up when difficulties arise.

The book became my therapy, and I started seeing things in a clearer light. I understood that years before, a shadow had embedded itself deep within my mind, like a virus. The best way to protect oneself from a virus is to let it enter your body in small doses, so the body becomes immune to it. Rather than fight it, I had to befriend it, and make it part of me so I could control the darkness and the negative thoughts and dispel the fear. Just as the best way to get rid of temptation is sometimes to give in before it becomes an obsession. I was thus able to identify the black shadow as the negative force that kept getting in the way of my fulfillment. I acknowledged and accepted it but swore it would never again possess me entirely.

I got over Nadia and the four years of torment she had put me through much more quickly than I had feared, and I focused on my children and the blessings they brought to my life, as well as my love of singing. My career took centre stage after I finally broke free of Nadia's hold. This time I didn't suffer the same self-doubt and despair over the breakup as I had when I left Anne-Marie. I may, however, have become more cynical about life in general and ever-more brash on stage.

In a review of my 2001 performance of Iago with the Montreal Opera, Arthur Kaptainis wrote in the Montreal Gazette, "Both the inner sneer of Quilico's tone, and the confidence with which he could even occupy a dark cranny left no doubt of his high calibre as a singing actor."

In *The Detroit News*, Lawrence B. Johnson wrote of my Don Giovanni performance,

"Anywhere the magnetic figure of this Don Giovanni, baritone Gino Quilico, appears onstage, that place becomes the drama epicentre. Virile, mysterious, suave, confident, that is Quilico's Don Giovanni."

There, Anne-Marie, skinny dorky bass, Maestro Gavazzani, father's second wife, Nadia, and all the bad reviewers, put that in your pipes and smoke it!

In 2003, I was awarded the Gold Record for my Novem recording of *Noel* in Quebec by L'association de l'industrie canadienne de l'enregistrement.

In a November 2003 interview in O, *The Oprah Magazine*, the legendary folksinger Joan Baez said this about the type of music that goes straight to her heart and gut:

> I have a desert island opera disc that I don't think many people know about in this country, *Le Secret* (Koch International) by singer Gino Quilico. There's something about his voice—he just moves me. You know how I would say it? Titi Robin moves me in the middle of my groin, and Gino Quilico moves me in the middle of my chest. Each note is like an intake of breath.

I revelled in my newfound independence and, on stage, strutted like a peacock again.

Chapter 38
On Don Giovanni

As usual, in between relationships, I yearned for the companionship of women. On stage as Rossini's Figaro, in one of the signature roles I have performed most frequently, I plotted lovers trysts, and as Don Giovanni, I seduced the ladies incessantly. Mozart based Don Giovanni on the legend of Don Juan, an immoral man and philanderer who stops at nothing to feed his sexual pleasures. Mozart had also reprised the character of Figaro, as a lover in his own right, in *The Marriage of Figaro* the year before he created *Don Giovanni*. The librettist of both his operas, Lorenzo da Ponte, was a rake himself and a close friend of Casanova. Some critics believe that Casanova had a hand in writing the last part of the Don Giovanni *libretto*. The story goes that when someone asked Casanova if he had seen the opera, he answered, "Seen it? I've lived it!"

Don Juan, Casanova, Don Giovanni, Figaro, all a bunch of super macho male characters! By today's standards they would justly be considered sexual predators and sociopaths, and most likely end up in jail. Though very much a product of the mores of their times, their actions cannot be considered less offensive or even less criminal today. Lately, I've had to take score and reflect on how my roles as Figaro and Don Giovanni, ones I have played with vim and vigour, should be perceived and played given our more progressive sensibilities towards sexual conduct and misconduct.

I always thoroughly researched the characters I played. For Don Giovanni, I read the original play by Tirso de Molina who introduced the character of Don Juan, later also portrayed by Molière, Byron, Dumas, and Shaw, to the world; I despised that character! In popular culture, Don Juan has even been romanticized as an insatiable lover, but the original portrayal is of a dark and evil man, a devious rapist with no qualms about murdering the male relatives of his female victims. Mozart's Don Giovanni may be a lighter, more palatable version of Don Juan, he is still a womanizer with a penchant for treating women like objects to collect and display. The Don does his share of despicable deeds, even murder, to satisfy his sex addiction, and so he can more easily seduce Donna Anna—the flavour of the moment. Being an *opera buffa, a dramma giocoso,* and at times treating his bed-hopping like a farce, the opera treads the fine line between comedy and tragedy. His friends gloss over his despicable actions, and they treat him more like an incurable lover of women than an abuser.

Does Mozart's opera glorify sexual exploitation? To the contrary, I believe that Mozart was ahead of his time in bringing this social evil to the attention of the public. The original title itself, *Il dissoluto punito, ossia il Don Giovanni*—literally *The Rake Punished, namely Don Giovanni*—should explain how Mozart viewed the man. Mozart is dead-on in conveying how a rake's immorality will only bring him damnation. In his music, Mozart gives the women a stronger voice than the men, a situation that gave me pause when it came on my own treatment of the women in my life. "*Pentiti, pentiti*/Repent, repent," Donna Elvira begs of don Giovanni. When he refuses to ask for forgiveness, the earth opens up beneath his feet, symbolizing his defeat. A statue of the murdered man drags him down to hell to be punished for all eternity for his behaviour towards women.

"And let him in flames atone," the chorus sings at the end.

I have been asked how today's opera world does with respect to sexual abuse and the treatment of women in general. Opera singers are very sexual, mainly because we deal with passions and emotions, and sex is always on people's brains. There's a lot of joking about sex and much gossip around the consensual affairs that spring up between singers and musicians. However, a few stories of sexual impropriety and even abuse involving prominent personalities have surfaced, but I do not believe that sexual abuse is as entrenched in opera culture as it is in the film and television industries.

There is no doubt that a few men in power have used their influence to satisfy their sexual proclivities. Over the decades, I witnessed well-known conductors and singers being singled out by both women and men as sexual predators, and some of these have finally been brought to justice. Why no one denounced them publicly earlier is a question that should make us reflect on our own collective complicity. The fact that it was tacitly tolerated demonstrates that our society had not evolved much in this respect since the days when the hyper-masculine behaviour of Casanova and Don Juan was glorified. Those named abusers deserved the scorn and judgments that they eventually received. Thanks to the awareness brought on by the testimony of some women, our eyes have been opened to how prevalent the problem has been in all spheres of society. Then there's someone like Placido Domingo who has also been accused of sexual harassment and who later apologized for his inappropriate behaviour. He, too, sought the ladies; some made themselves available to him, others did not welcome his advances, but I find it hard to identify him as an abuser who preyed on vulnerable women. I see him more as an incurable Don Giovanni without the crime. However, we've learned since that the line between the actions of a sexual abuser and that of an old-world ladies' man is indeed very thin.

The Harvey Weinsteins of Hollywood and other powerful men have been exposed for using their power to advance or end the careers of their victims. The incidence of abuse in the opera world is much lower, maybe because we are fewer in number, but also because of the nature of the business. Natural talent, skill, and training are essential pre-conditions in classical music and opera. Even a sex-crazed conductor, maestro, or lead singer cannot play with these crucial qualities in refusing or granting favours. Opera requires too much. You can't get a major role because you slept with the conductor if you don't have the voice, the experience, and the background. The same applies to the use of enhancement drugs. There are no performance drugs to help a singer reach a high C. Drugs would have a disastrous effect on the absolute need for concentration, which is crucial to remembering lines, keeping tempo, and coordinating body movements. One sings with the brain as much as the voice box, and it must be kept on high alert, not half-dimmed by drugs.

In Don Giovanni's famous aria in Act 1, known as the "Catalogue Aria," Leporello, Giovanni's servant, reads from his little black book and lists his master's 1003 conquests in Spain alone. Following my last painful relationship with one woman and after incarnating the incurable lover on stage, I, too, tried to emulate his mission of conquering as many women as possible. It was not out of lust, rather a deeply felt need for connection. And this is also what makes Mozart's Don Giovanni a richer more ambiguous character than just a superficial Latin lover. In searching for endless women, he hungers for the ideal image of the love that eludes him. Despite my previous failed relationships, I still believed in women and craved the support they could offer me. Was this an egotistical need? It would still take me a while to face that question. What I most embraced in the Figaro and the Don Giovanni characters was their love of life and their praise of women. Don Giovanni sings, *"Vivan le femmine, viva il buon vino* ! / *Sostegno e gloria d'umanità/* Long live women and wine, support and glory of humankind." In other words, I never stopped yearning for love and a celebration of life!

Chapter 39
Sara

I played Don Giovanni so often that, in time, I became blasé to the groupies who followed me after each performance and readily offered themselves with a simple nod of the head. I knew they were not after me, but the role I had just sung and the fleeting excitement of having slept with a Don Giovanni. My own catalogue aria that saw women as numbers left me unfulfilled and I became increasingly bored with the scene. Did these women ever wonder what Gino was all about? Did they care about my past struggles, my fears, my pains, and my dreams for the future? I wanted to be with someone who wanted me for myself. In my search for women, or was it wholeness, I went incognito.

Technology has always fascinated me, and as a product of the digital age, I learned that one could cast one's net over a larger pool without ever leaving one's bedroom. I discovered online dating when it was still considered taboo by the general population. I revelled in presenting myself under a false name, revealing my photo only to the most exciting possibilities. And even then, I didn't reveal what I did for a living. I discovered how small the reach of the opera world really is within the general population, and even if somewhat disappointed that none of the women I met recognized my name, I considered online dating a new-found game that distracted me in between performances while providing the lure of endless unknown possibilities for a dreamer like me.

"*Figaro qua Figaro là*," I sang on stage, while in my free time, I surfed the internet for my conquests. I did not treat the dating sites as meat market venues. I could have frequented night clubs for that. I was polite, respectful, and honest with the ladies I met. In June of 2004, a photo of a Black woman named Sara with delicate features and a tender smile immediately caught my attention. It took me a while before I contacted her, but her enigmatic Mona Lisa smile attracted me. I finally clicked on "send message" and asked for a date. We spoke on the phone a few times before meeting for coffee. When I gave her my real name, I was grateful that she didn't recognize it. We exchanged stories of the many funny meetings we both had with people who misrepresented their ages by posting photos of their younger selves. She told me of one incident when she met a man who did not have any teeth. On my way to our first date, I stopped by a costume shop I knew, and when I met her, I opened my mouth to flash a false set of rotten teeth. We laughed throughout our get-togethers, and in internet dating parlance, we "clicked."

Sara Decayette was born in Haiti and came to Montreal with her parents when she was two years old. In the 70s, many in Haiti escaped the dictatorship of Papa Doc Duvalier and poor job opportunities, some emigrating to the United States, many to Quebec because they spoke French and felt welcome here. Her family settled in the suburb of Longueuil, on the south shore of Montreal, the only Black family in that neighbourhood. Two brothers would later be born in Quebec. Her father, a mechanic for the Canadian Pacific Railway, was not very present in their lives. He was a womanizer and a manipulator, and her mother eventually divorced him. Sara remembers spending time in a woman's shelter with her mother to get away from the abusive relationship. After her fragile mother married another man with the same philandering ways, Sara helped her break the destructive pattern. With strength of character and helped by her faith, her mother put herself through school to become a patient attendant, and worked hard to support the family and to make sure her children received a good education. Sara graduated from university with a Bachelor of Commerce and chose to work in the social assistance department of the Quebec provincial government.

With such poor male role models in her youth, Sara believed she had to rely on herself and was over-cautious about men and marriage when she met me. She had also just ended a relationship with a manic-depressive man and her online-dating experience had not been very promising.

When I showed up with the false teeth, I put her at ease, and she dropped her defenses, smiling broadly. She knew nothing of opera except that her last companion listened to Baroque music, which did nothing to enliven their joyless relationship. After our first date, she later confessed, she called an Italian friend to ask if she had heard of me. Once she ascertained I had not misrepresented myself, she happily accepted a second date. Because she had had to struggle through some difficult times, the philosophy of "don't sweat the small stuff" is one she lives by. I liked that she was easygoing, always in a good mood, and did everything possible to fit into my still busy life. With her, I felt a sense of order after the chaos and disorder of my life of the last years, but as I had given up on marriage and life-long relationships, I did not promise her more than I could offer at that time. Moreover, I was expending all my energy on reinventing myself in more ways than one.

My life with Sara coincided with the start of some new unexpected but exciting projects. One day, I received a phone call from a famous Quebec pop singer, René Simard, who was directing a show, Célébration, at the Casino de Gatineau—a show intended to promote the newly formed Loto-Québec. During the show, an MC would draw the winning numbers for the current lottery in front of a live audience of over a thousand people. There was entertainment in between the draws and performances by well-known Quebec artists.

René's request for my participation in one of the shows took me by surprise, and my first impulse was to refuse. On the phone, I put on my best, snobby, big opera divo act. I felt that performing in a casino in Gatineau, of all places, across the river from Ottawa was beneath my status after singing in all the world's major opera houses. But then, for fun, I thought I'd "shoot the moon." Neil Shicoff and I used to play a card game called Hearts. If a card looked good, you'd shoot the moon, or you'd go for it. So, I shot the moon with a request for a high fee to sing for Loto-Québec, thinking they would refuse. To my surprise, they agreed without any negotiation. René proposed I sing a medley with another Quebec pop singer Sylvain Cossette. I accepted on the condition that Sylvain venture into my musical world and sing an aria from *Figaro*.

At the first rehearsal, the three of us were taken aback at how our voices blended to perfection. At the show, we sang "Caruso" by Lucio Dalla in Italian, "Que je t'aime" by Johnny Hallyday In French, "Rhapsody" by Queen in English, and ended with "Largo al Factotum" from *The Barber of Seville* by Rossini. The event was an absolute triumph that earned a standing ovation.

Later, Simard confessed that he had never heard of me before someone mentioned my name to him. I only knew of him because I remembered that my first wife, Anne-Marie, had danced in a show with him before I even became an opera singer. René was a child superstar who sang with Frank Sinatra. The pop and opera worlds are truly two separate entities, and as much as we scoff at the pop singers, they fill the stadiums and couldn't care less about our high-brow pretensions. Luciano Pavarotti was the first classical artist to successfully bridge these two worlds.

A few days after the show, Guy Cloutier, whom I would learn was a famous Quebec producer, contacted me about recording a duet with a young 13-year-old girl, Marilou. I had no clue who either of them was, but I accepted. My meeting with Simard had softened my stance against the pop music scene. The recording was my first solo Christmas CD called NOEL. The music to the song had been written by two Italian composers over fifty years earlier. European artist Dalida had already recorded the Italian version, and Sarah Brightman, the English. We released the French version, "Je serai là pour toi," in November 2004. The CD went Gold with over 50,000 copies sold and surprisingly made me more recognizable in Québec than all of my opera performances thus far. The release of that CD was the beginning of what would bring my name to the attention of the pop world.

After that heady experience, I realized that my early teenage enthusiasm for experimenting with rock, though unsuccessful at the time, had never entirely left me. I saw this as a new adventure, but, in the beginning, it still represented a distraction in between the more serious opera roles. That fall, I also sang Iago in *Otello* in Malmo Sweden and had opera bookings all across Europe.

In my love life with Sara, I sensed that she was looking for a serious relationship. There was too much going on in my professional life, and I did not want the extra pressure of a committed relationship. However, I loved her enough not to want to hurt her—I had made that mistake before—and so in December of that year, before leaving for Paris, I broke up with her. I was conflicted, knowing how well we had clicked, and it was just before Christmas so I realized that I had broken her heart, but I needed the time away to rethink my personal life.

Chapter 40
Crossing Over

The event that further skyrocketed my pop career happened in the fall of 2004, before my breakup with Sara. Ironically, it was the result of an invitation from the Montreal Symphony Orchestra, the OSM, to audition for a role in a new classical version of the cyberpunk opera *Starmania* by Michel Berger and Luc Plamondon. Once again, I wanted to pull my divo act and tell them I was way past auditioning for people, least of all for a pop opera, but first I called some friends to investigate Luc Plamondon. I learned that he was a big name in Quebec and France, so I put my pride in my pocket and auditioned for the role I thought was right for my voice range. I sang the hit song "J'aurais voulu être un artiste." I could tell that this selection did not impress Mr. Plamondon. He handed me another sheet of music scored with extremely high notes—more of a tenor part for the role of bad boy Johnny Roquefort. I am a baritone but have a facility with high notes especially in the falsetto range. Behind Mr. Plamondon's trade-mark dark glasses, I could see his eyebrows rise in excitement. He immediately stopped my singing after only a few phrases and said, "You are my Johnny." Unable to help myself I responded, "Since I am Italian, can we change the name from Johnny Roquefort to Johnny Parmigiano?" He was not amused by my making light of his opera, but nevertheless we shook hands like gentlemen! Despite my misplaced request, we remain good friends to this day, and I sang in the classical version of *Starmania* in Montreal at Place des

Arts with the OSM. In December of 2004, after breaking up with Sara, I left for Paris to bring the show at the Palais des Congrès, not far from where I had last lived in that city. *Starmania* is now considered one of the most famous French rock operas.

All this meant adjustments to my singing techniques and a fair amount of stress to handle the new demands of the pop world. As odd as this may sound, the first thing I had to learn was how to handle a microphone. As opera singers we have a lot of power in our voices and don't need microphones. Our constant concern is the ability to project without one, whereas the microphone is an essential instrument for pop singers. I had to learn to place my mouth close to the microphone only when concentrating more on the interpretation of the words and focus on the subtle nuances of the voice. When going for the high notes I had to pull away from it, or I'd blow it up.

After returning from France, several months passed before I called Sara and asked her on a date. In all that time, I had not stopped thinking about her. I asked her to join me in Austin, Texas, where in April 2005, I sang in *The Marriage of Figaro*. My call took her by surprise. When I invited her, I sensed a nervousness in her voice as if uncertain on whether to take my offer seriously. She told me later, she was afraid I'd break her heart again, but she accepted. It was the first time that Sara would see me perform in a full opera. She had a hard time following the opera, even though she'd bought a book to read about the plotline. But the sight of me in costume and the chance to come backstage to meet the rest of the cast impressed her. She has since become hooked on the music, the rituals and the spectacle of opera, realizing that there's more to it than plotline.

We spent a lot of time together that summer. We talked about me taking on more crossover contracts. I decided to hire an agent to promote me in this new world, and he immediately found me a project with Rick Alison—the ex-husband of famous singer Lara Fabian. Rick asked that I record an album of his songs with him. However, my association with Luc Plamondon was still strong, and I asked him to collaborate with us for the album as well. The album entitled *Un jour une nuit,* includes two selections with Plamondon's lyrics, "À travers toutes les femmes" and "Danse mon Esmeralda" from his successful musical *Notre Dame de Paris.*

Things were moving fast, and I realized that I could live a more normal life singing closer to home. Following the recording, I jumped at the invitation from Luc Plamondon to play my next role, that of Quasimodo in *Notre Dame de Paris* at the Bell Centre. The musical based on Victor Hugo's novel *Notre Dame de Paris/The Hunchback of Notre Dame* with music by Riccardo Cocciante and lyrics by Plamondon had been performed worldwide in different languages since its debut in Paris in 1998. It had also enjoyed the most successful first year of any musical ever. Luc was now bringing it to a Quebec audience..

All 21 shows of the Montreal debut in June 2005 sold out in a few days. The role, set in my favourite city of Paris, turned out to be another incredible adventure. The hunchback Quasimodo being a very physical role, I had to train every day with dancers who were half acrobats. The stage was the largest I had ever performed on, and I had to run from one end to the other half bent forward like a hunchback—not the most relaxed position for my back. They had me climbing up and down a 40-foot wall with safety harnesses and rolling upside down on stage with my feet and arms attached to a huge wheel. I joked that my next audition would be for the Cirque de Soleil. I grinned and bared lots of back pain on that wheel, but the production was exhilarating. Before going on stage, I had two hours of makeup, and this for 21 performances in 23 days. An energy drink, which sponsored the show, helped me get through every night.

I had become my own version of the tragic Rigoletto, another hunchback with a curse on his head and the role that most reminded me of my father.

Luc would say later about my crossover style: *"Chanteur d'opera qui chante la chanson… parce-que je pense que quand il chante la chanson c'est naturel—c'est un chanteur….quoi./*He's an opera singer that sings songs… because I think that when he sings songs, it's natural… he's a singer, that's all."

From that point onwards, Sara and I were never apart, and although she had her own apartment in Montreal, she practically lived with me and my son Enrico who had also chosen to live with me. After a few months, it didn't seem logical to pay two rents. In September of that year, she sublet her apartment, and moved in with me. Though yet not ready to commit to another marriage, I found myself constantly thinking about the future and how I could spend more time at home.

When I was away, I spent hours on Skype talking to Sara. She offered me comfort when from near and far—the antithesis of Nadia. I was happy to have her back in my life. At the same time, my routine of travelling the globe, happy to be alternating classical opera with lighter performances, continued.

In the fall of 2005, I played Don Giovanni in Seoul Korea. The public loved my performance and gave me standing ovations. One evening as I looked into the audience and saw thousands of smiling Korean faces, together with a sense of appreciation, I also felt a strong sense of estrangement. I couldn't recognize a single person in that audience. I thought to myself, *Here I am being treated like a superstar by the public as well as the director, and there is no one at my side with whom to share this moment. After this scene of adulation, I will be sleeping all alone in a hotel room, my clothes half unpacked in my suitcase.* While being driven by a personal driver to a 5-star hotel, thoughts of the loneliness of an opera singer's life intensified. *When the glamour is gone and the show is over, I am not Don Giovanni, but a man alone in a hotel room far from home and far from anyone who knows and really loves him.*

Luckily, Korea is thirteen hours ahead, so I connected with Sara by Skype when I got into my hotel. After we said goodbye, I spoke out loud, "What am I doing miles away from a woman I love, night after night? What kind of life is this?" I looked for a pen and paper and poured out my feelings on the page. When I finished writing, a sudden sense of freedom overtook me. I resolved to make some crucial changes in my life and not repeat the patterns that had destroyed my previous personal relationships. I started thinking seriously about how to cut down on my travel but still perform. To keep my promise, I had the text I had written framed, and I hung it above my desk in my home office.

While still honouring previous engagements, *Otello* in Portland, *Carmen* in Finland, *Elisir* in Monte Carlo, I asked my agent to stop booking me far from home. She warned me that this would cut down considerably on available singing roles and suggested doing more recitals—a scarier proposition than I had ever thought.

Singing an opera on stage is certainly more demanding, but there is an entire entourage of people and props to support the role: the costumes, the chorus, the ballet, and the stage settings to make you forget yourself. The role takes over, and you become Figaro, Iago, Marcello, Escamillo, Don Giovanni. The mask gives you confidence, and you hide behind it. In a recital, you are alone, naked in front of an audience. It took a few recitals before I felt comfortable in this new form, but I quickly came to like the intimacy that it provided.

Encouraged by Sara, the concept of singing more crossover music took shape and form. My agent soon booked me for a 2008 production of *Les Misérables* in Quebec City. After making important decisions for my career, I felt that my life had taken a new turn. I was excited about the prospects to sing and record with less stress and fewer obligations to tie me down. I saw myself spending happy days in my backyard in Beaconsfield, a suburb of Montreal, with Sara and my son, Enrico; my daughter, Sofia, still resided with Kathryn. I was happy in this new arrangement, though still not ready to pledge a death-do-us-part formal union with Sara.

Then out of nowhere, my worst nightmare came true, and my whole world crashed and halted for six months.

Chapter 41
The Crash

My son Enrico had been a fun-loving kid throughout his teen years, and when he came to live with me in his twenties, he fit seamlessly into my and Sara's lives, except that like many young men, he did not always like do his chores. I had to be the parent from time to time, a responsibility I will admit I am less cut out for. Enrico was born in Paris and had travelled the world from an early age and developed some sophisticated tastes. When we lived in London, one of his teachers claimed that our son was either lying or had a great imagination. Enrico had told her his favourite food was smoked salmon and mussels, unusual choices for most kids his age in London at that time. He eventually became more North American, and his tastes included burgers and fries. He smoked a pack of cigarettes a day, liked to party, and probably drank too much. In addition, he owned a used car that we bought together and always had part-time jobs while he studied. Like me at his age, he didn't shy away from pumping gas or washing windows to make extra money. Being an exceptionally social individual, he enjoyed working in service and sales at restaurants and retail stores. He kept fit by exercising regularly at the downtown YMCA.

I watched him develop into a bright, intelligent, and creative young man, physically fit and dandily dressed. His pastimes included activities you would expect from any twenty-three-year-old guy: going out with friends, taking care of his car, spending time with his girlfriend, and going for rides on his father's motorcycle. Like me, he had developed a love of motorized vehicles. I allowed him to use my motorcycle more freely than I should have.

Life caught up with him at 100 km/h.

What could be worse for a parent than getting a call to hear that your son has been rushed to the trauma unit of a hospital with a severe head injury and is in a coma after a crash on the bike you let him use?

I received the call from the police in the early evening of May 21ˢᵗ, 2006. The officer was phoning from the Lakeshore General Hospital in the West Island of Montreal. They instructed me to go directly to the ICU at the Montreal General Hospital, where they were bringing my son. He was in an induced coma to limit any brain activity considered disruptive to the healing of an injury of that magnitude. What injury? What magnitude? I couldn't quite register what they had just told me. They had been speaking so quickly.

By the time I arrived at the hospital, they had inserted a shunt in his skull—a shunt is a tube, they explained, to help drain cerebrospinal fluid. Unfortunately, the procedure had not stopped the swelling inside his skull. There was one final procedure to try, they told me: a craniotomy. His brain was swelling so much that the blood had only one place to go, downward. With too much excessive pressure on his cerebral cortex, he would lose all mental functioning, or need life-support. Besides the brain trauma, he had broken ribs, a fractured pelvis, and his left arm was completely shattered and had to be put back together with pins and screws. The only procedure that could alleviate the pressure on his brain and let him live was to remove half of his skull.

Harrowed and stunned, his mother and I had to make a swift life or death decision. We put our money on Rico.

Thanks to early decisive actions on the part of the doctors, the procedure was successful, and the pressure dissipated, but he remained in a coma. I talked to him constantly so that he wouldn't lose his connection to life. As in the clinic when he was born, I played Mozart for him, I never wanted to leave his side, sleeping in his room on a lounge chair, unshaven for days until all the ladies ganged up on me and forced me to go home for a shower. I watched over him continually and even lightly touched his exposed brain wondering what my son would be like once he came out of his induced coma. When he did three weeks later, I was mentally ready to face the next challenges. They moved him from the ICU to the 11th floor of the Montreal General Hospital and he spent two months there undergoing various operations needed to heal his other significant injuries. During the three weeks of coma, he lost 70 pounds, and he was a slim man to begin with. But above all, he had lost touch with reality.

Throughout the long ordeal, Kathryn and Sofia never wavered in keeping our hopes alive, and luckily, I also had Sara by my side, who, with her quiet support, helped keep the fear and despair from overwhelming me. Though I had had many dark moments of depression, the shadow that had threatened me at other difficult moments in my life never had a chance with these three wonderful women at my side. People's true colours surface at times like these. Sofia cancelled her summer classes to be at her brother's bedside; Kathryn was solicitous and caring; Sara was loving and present. Our only concern was for Rico. The remainder of 2006 was all about his rehabilitation. He had to learn the most basic life skills: walking, dressing, pronouncing words, telling time, tying his shoes, remembering, feeling, and so much more.

Small miracles truly saved Rico. Two doctors happened to be in the car behind him when a speeding vehicle crossed the highway illegally, causing him to lose control of the motorcycle, and crash head-first against the car that cut him off.

They called the ambulance and tended to him with the proper care in those first vital moments after the accident. The doctors at the hospital made the correct swift decisions, and I cannot emphasize enough the precious contributions of the incredible nurses!

It was early summer, so I didn't have any major engagements. I had a few concerts here and there within the province of Québec in August of that year but refused whatever new projects came my way because I didn't have the heart to perform or sing.

Sofia stayed at Enrico's side for hours on end. She would bake fresh brownies for the nurses. "I want them to be happy," she'd say. I was so grateful that she had grown into such a compassionate and loving daughter and sister.

Sofia had always been a very studious young lady, never carried away by the adolescent stuff like cigarettes, nightclubs, etc. This was her choice and was very refreshing for me. One of her weaknesses is shoes, but I believe this is a very common woman's thing. To my great pleasure, she loved music as a child, sang and studied the piano, and has sung with me on several occasions. She also played basketball and badminton. She and Enrico have always been good friends. They talk to each other a lot and support each other in their day-to-day lives. But Sofia is a perfectionist, and from time to time, we butt heads. I met my match when it came to stubborn behaviours, and I rarely won battles with her. She is a Leo, and I am a Taurus. My head is harder, but her bite is more ferocious.

The first time that I felt able to sing again was for a private event which I had committed to and could not cancel. I asked Sofia to sing the duo of *The Prayer* with me. We went to the hospital first. I changed into my tuxedo in the bathroom of Enrico's room and Sofia donned her evening dress. We told Rico that we were going to sing, and in a soft voice, he said, "Have fun." We walked down the hill from the Montreal General Hospital to the Ritz-Carlton Hotel in our evening clothes. It all felt so magical, singing together with my daughter and then returning to Enrico's side and finding him sleeping peacefully! I will never forget that moment when my daughter and I prayed together in song for Enrico's return to full life. We repeated *The Prayer* when Rico was discharged from the hospital and was well enough to come see us sing a concert in the Lanaudiere Music Festival. Both Sofia and I were moved to tears.

By January 2007, I had already started to sing again regularly. My first extended contract was to sing in *Carmen* in Savonlinna, Finland, from June 15th to July 15th.

Physically, things improved quickly for Enrico. A year later, he had more or less recuperated on a physical level: his shattered arm had mended, his skull flap was put back with screws, but his cognitive rehabilitation took longer. He was moved from the hospital to the Montreal Rehabilitation Centre and finally to the Constance Lethbridge Centre, as an outpatient, to continue tackling the next difficult challenges.

One would think that once Enrico's injuries healed and after rehabilitation, life would return to what it was before the crash, but Enrico had to deal with a difficult consequence of his type of accident: depression. It would take years before found his direction again. The family continued to care for him and support him while he relived the trauma of the crash. He had nightmares and suffered from PTSD. Sometimes, I felt as if my life had also been put on hold.

Depression is a common long-term complication after a severe Traumatic Brain Injury, TBI. On a personal level, this was extremely hard to deal with and was territory I did not want to revisit. Depression had paralyzed me and made me lose myself for short periods, but I rose above it each time. My son's depression was a different animal to tame because it was caused by severe physiological changes in the brain. I feared that he'd have to deal with this debilitating condition for the rest of his life. Because I understood the pain of depression first-hand, it was doubly hard to imagine this mindset lasting a lifetime for Enrico.

With great anxiety, I read that the prognosis for many people who have sustained this level of brain injury is not promising. Patients may be unable to return to full-time employment and may lose significant relationships. These types of accidents often come with impairments that prevent a person from functioning in their daily lives. It hurt me to know that there was little I or the family could do beyond offering emotional support.

I started filtering my opera contracts, resolving to commit to the crossover world, though it was already in the works after the various successes I had enjoyed. The timing was right. I refused a few engagements in Europe, and this allowed me to spend more time at home to breathe and plan my new direction. I refused some important proposals, including one from the Metropolitan Opera—and one never refuses the Met. Looking back, it may have been a mistake on my part because New York is an easy flight from Montreal, but at the time, I could not get excited about the roles offered, and I was tired of the pressures and the politics of the opera world, the jockeying for lead roles, the travelling, the eating in restaurants, the sleeping in fancy hotels with no soul. Staying home was a welcome escape that suited me just fine. I realized how often I had resolved to cut down on traveling–the downside of my career–yet had never been able to say "no" to the thrill of the performances when the roles were offered. Now, I needed some normality, and there is nothing like almost losing your child to bring you closer to your personal truth.

Chapter 42
Musical Journeys

While dealing with my son's slow rehabilitation, a dear friend Steven Mercurio called me one day and said, "Hey Gino, how would you like to sing in paradise for a week?" Coming from Steve, I believed the hyperbole. Steve and I had shared many exciting projects, and I trusted his musical acumen. I said yes, no questions asked.

Sometimes you meet people in your life that just click. Steve was one of those people. I first made his acquaintance when he conducted some of my mother's *Water for Africa* fundraising concerts. Then I met him in New York on the world premiere of *Ghosts of Versailles*, when he had worked on many of the musical arrangements for the composer John Carigliano. In 1993, soon after my mother's death, we were just two young guys making music with passion and love—no ego trips between us. Our connection was simply put, music and friendship. He had also gotten along very well with my mother during their collaboration, both of them driven by a desire to give back to society through a love of music

Besides being a conductor, Steven is also a composer in his own right, a musical arranger, an eclectic musician, and so much more. He loves collecting original Bugs Bunny designs, musical scores and, like me, played electric guitar in his youth—a Fender Stratocaster, I believe. We became friends immediately, both seeing ourselves as a little different from many in the stiffer, uptight opera crowd. Steve has conducted all over the world, including the three tenors, Andrea Bocelli, Sting, and so many more. Under his direction, I also sang in *Eugene Onegin* in Philadelphia and *Don Giovanni* in Detroit.

In 2002, he brought me to Palermo, Sicily, to sing in Gershwin's *Lady in the Dark* at the Teatro Massimo where the last Godfather trilogy was filmed. In the 90s, we also performed together on a cruise ship, *The Marmoz*, after an invitation from Barbara Hendricks and her husband, my agent. This ship had a long tradition of presenting orchestras with distinguished musicians and soloists. We sang outdoor concerts at different ports, but best of all, I got to spend time together with good friends, in a stress-free atmosphere.

Badly in need of a get-away after Enrico's ordeal, I was happy to accept the "paradise" Steve offered: an all-expense-paid vacation to sing in Puccini's *La Fanciulla del West*, on the island of Saint-Barthelemy for the following January. Also referred to as Saint Barth and a playground for the rich and famous, the island offers the perfect antidote for the Canadian winter blues. The yearly Classical Music Festival Steve conducts in Saint Barth offers opera, jazz, and chamber music concerts with internationally renowned artists and musicians in the churches of Lorient and Gustavia.

None of us needed long rehearsal time since Steve invited only seasoned singers and top-notch musicians from major world orchestras such as The Metropolitan Opera Orchestra, The San Francisco Opera, The Chicago Lyric, The Montreal Symphony Orchestra, and so on. We were all there to have a good time and play and sing glorious Puccini under a splendid Caribbean sky.

No paradise is complete without someone that you love next to you. Fortunately, I had Sara with me, and this is where I first admired her beautiful body, her skin shining like black velour against the brilliant blue waters of the sea. She looked so beautiful to me; I could not believe my luck to have such a gorgeous woman in my life. I fell in love all over again. We explored the island on a Vespa scooter, we hiked and visited every corner, tried countless restaurants, and got many mosquito bites. Even with the pesky insects, Saint Barth was magical.

Once as we were walking on the beach, two paparazzi came from hiding in a bush with a camera. Maybe they thought we might be famous actors or personalities. Once they realized we were just simple folks, they left. It was an anti-climatic moment, but it was hilarious! We had a good laugh about not being famous enough to make it on the cover of *People* magazine.

During the day, we'd cross paths with other singers and musicians on the beaches and at the bars. Some evenings, I would also sing an aria or two with the all-star orchestra. It was heavenly. The woman responsible for the music festival, Frances Debroff, was first violinist of the Pittsburg orchestra and has a beautiful home in Saint Barth. She organizes the event in January every year. Initially, it was very modest but has become more popular, and Steve has brought it to another level. Since he took charge, it has become unlike any experience I have ever had in music. As relaxed as we could all be, we were there to make music in its purest form!

Since that first experience, Steve has invited me to Saint Barth four more times to sing in *Manon, Madama Butterly*, and twice in my very favourite *La Bohème*—always Puccini. What could be closer to paradise than singing Puccini in blissful Saint Barth!

On my return, I became more resolved than ever to reduce my opera contracts, cut down on travelling, and essentially terminate my international career. It occurred to me that one can travel far through imagination and music. The original idea started when I sang a mix of musical selections about my travels around the world, a concept I presented at the Canadian Embassy in San Francisco for Prime Minister Kim Campbell. I had not yet given the concert a name. It was a conventional classical concert where the singer comes on stage, sings, bows, but does not speak to the audience. I began the evening singing as planned, in the traditional way, when suddenly I made a mistake in the score, which made me hesitate. To cover up the blunder, I started to talk to the audience about the memories the song had solicited. The effect was so satisfying to me that I continued to do so throughout the evening. The audience loved it, and I realized that I had a story to tell.

The experience inspired me to create a hybrid of a show and a concert, *Voyage Musical,* that involved opening up to the audience about the personal meaning of each piece I sang. The instrumentalists were a classical pianist and a pop pianist on an electronic keyboard who handled the backup sounds, such as violins, accordions, or whatever sounds we needed to augment the vocals. Next, I managed, with an agent, to get a concert tour in Quebec. But before going on tour, I rethought and experimented with the concept and the musical approach until I decided to hire two electronic keyboard players in addition to a guitarist. The two keyboard players, Manu Pitois and Toni Carlone shared the backup music and the musical effects, and the guitarist, Daniel Marsolais, gave the production a more popular feel. We first took the show on the road, not in huge trucks loaded with electronic equipment like rock stars, but in a Dodge Caravan packed with guitars, electronic keyboards, and the four of us. It was like I had gone back in time to my teen years. Here was Gino Quilico, the globe-trotting opera singer, now singing in remote places like Chicoutimi, Abitibi, and other small towns I had never heard of, at times schlepping through catastrophic snowstorms. As we arrived at the theatres with our small caravan, I would unload with the help of the musicians and the technicians and assist them in setting up the stage. It was like a whole new career and experience. Sara was hands-on and provided vital help throughout the preparation, the drives, and during the shows. Where I saw complications, she offered solutions. Sharing my experience with the public and returning home soon after every show was the payback for all the inconveniences of this new adventure.

Then I prepared for a role that had a further transformative effect on my life.

Chapter 43
Jean Valjean:
Redemption and Hope

By some divine intervention, I found myself singing the extraordinary character of Jean Valjean, with whom I found much common ground. It was Sofia who had encouraged me to take on the role. She loved the musical *Les Misérables,* and I accepted the challenge because of her nudge. I was so thankful to God for giving my son a second chance and for giving me such a wonderful daughter and Sara as a companion.

I related to Jean Valjean on many levels, not the least of which was the city where the story unfolds and which had played such a profound role in my own life. It's where the allure of the spectacle of opera began, where I experienced my own bohemian beginning as an artist, where I tasted my first thrill of fame and my biggest successes, and where my son was born.

I got deep into character from the very beginning of rehearsals. I wanted to understand Jean Valjean not only to play the role I was paid to perform but to understand the man and possibly myself.

Jean Valjean is a complicated character, living a twistedly complex existence. He has stolen bread to feed his family and is a prisoner, a victim of violence, and a man on the run shunned by society. And because of a rare kindness from a bishop, he goes on to become a benefactor before he is forced to become a fugitive again. We first see him as a very angry man because of his misfortunes, which force him to create his many identities. At a certain point, he must confront who he is.

He asks, "Who am I? Can I conceal myself from everyone? Pretend I'm not the man I was before? And must my name, until I die, be no more than an alibi?" In so doing, he also must confront his fears and demons.

Jean Valjean lived another life in another Paris. I never experienced even remotely the cruelty that the society of his time inflicted on him, but he still spoke to me. I was a professional opera singer blinded by the obsessive goal of an international career. I may not have been as angry as him, but nonetheless, I had striven to find my true self while living in a dream world until it was abruptly interrupted by my son's tragic accident. The world of opera, the race for fame and glory, are exhilarating, but in the end, it's not real and not a place in which to get lost. Valjean reinvents himself and makes a conscious effort to redeem his sins, selflessly devoting his life to help others and confessing his identity to save another man.

Love, compassion, and faith became the essential values in his life, and this awareness changed me tremendously. The prayer that Jean Valjean sings, "Let me die and let him live," was a prayer I had expressed to God many times over right after my son's accident, "Please let me die and give my son a chance to live his youthful life."

> The summers die
> One by one,
> How soon they fly
> On and on
> And I am old
> And will be gone.
> Bring him peace
> Bring him joy
> He is young,
> He is only a boy.
> You can take,
> You can give
> Let him be
> Let him live.

Two years after the accident, I prayed that my son would resume a normal happy life, that he would regain the enthusiasm and joie de vivre that life had had in store for him but that had been snatched away. It happened in an instant; it was a moment of distraction while riding free against the wind, a sensation I myself had sought while riding that same bike. Miracles had already happened, and I prayed for more each night I sang.

Little by little, it was Enrico himself who by consistently challenging himself academically, professionally, and physically produced more small miracles. In his own words, "When I say a long recovery, you might think months, weeks, a long couple of days, but I am still to this day recovering."

I learned to accept that his full recovery would take time—and to rejoice in the incremental improvements he made on his strength of character. His earlier love of physical exercise led him to undertake studies with a mission not only to overcome his limitations but to use his knowledge to help others. He became a teacher, completed a Masters in Adapted Physical Activity at McGill, and pursued a PhD in Rehabilitation Science at the University of Toronto, where he developed a community-based physical activity program for adults with traumatic brain injury (TBI).

Physical exercise was the biggest contributing factor in allowing Enrico to recover physically, excel in his studies and make a full recovery. I am not qualified to explain the details the research, but what I do know is that it has brought balance and purpose to his life. Furthermore, he has become a public speaker and advocate for traumatic brain injury awareness.

I am inspired by his message of hope. "I feel that by doing my work and living my life to the fullest, I am offering hope to those suffering from TBI. There are many stages that you go through in the long journey to recovery—some of them dark. Despite the odds, others can also have positive outcomes."

I had had the start of an epiphany in Korea while facing an adoring but anonymous audience, which had already made me question what kind of life I wanted. Playing Jean Valjean made me connect further with my truth and especially my heart. It was the final affirmation that I had to make real changes in my life and that I needed to re-invent myself.

Ultimately, it's Jean Valjean's love for his adopted daughter, Cossette, that changes the man into a real human being. This love made me more aware of the gift of love that my own daughter, Sofia, and my family represent.

While immersed in my role in *Les Misérables* at the Théâtre Capitole in Quebec City, I had to put an end to *Voyage Musical*. Jean Pilote, the director of the Capitole, who was responsible for the musical, asked me to put together a Valentine's Day concert in February 2009. I followed the model of the musical voyages to create *Serata d'Amore,* an appropriate theme for Valentine's Day. To encourage the up-and-coming Quebec talents, I invited a young singer from *Les Misérables* to sing alongside Sofia. Dominic Boulianne, the pianist from Les Miz, joined the mix with a trio of classically-trained musicians he had formed. TrioSphere was made up of the pianist Dominic, a violinist, Lizann Gervais, and a cellist, Elisabeth Giroux. We developed a relationship that lasted many years. *Serata d'Amore* was a progression of *Voyage Musical,* but more refined with better stories and much closer to the classical approach of my work. I could now tell stories about my family and the people I worked with, such as Pavarotti, Luc Plamondon, and others. Our first show was at the Saint Sauveur Summer Festival. Again, it was a tremendous success and as *Les Misérables* came to an end in the summer of 2010, I continued the concept of *Serata D'Amore by* selecting romantic arias in combination with popular songs that spoke of love in all its forms.

Jean Valjean finds love and compassion at the end. I also found love in my family and the people that had been around me through Enrico's recovery. Jean Valjean provided personal therapy for me after my son's accident. I relived the experience every night of the 150 nights that I sang the famous prayer "Bring him home." Bring my son home, give him another chance at a happy life. I found a new appreciation for all the gifts life had given me and the life I was now living and prayed that my son would be accorded the same.

Most of all, what Jean Valjean gave me was the inspiration to change as an artist and as a man. One can make many errors and lose oneself through the pursuits of life, but life can also give you many chances to redeem yourself, and a new life is always possible. What is success, fame if not accompanied by love and the realization that your work has some-how contributed to making this world a better place for those around you? Elusive dreams that, once you wake up, slip from your fingers in the bat of an eye.

Victor Hugo himself, whose profound story inspired the musical, wrote towards the end of the novel:

The book which the reader has before him at this moment is, from one end to the other, in its entirety and details... a progress from evil to good, from injustice to justice, from falsehood to truth, from night to day, from appetite to conscience, from corruption to life; from bestiality to duty, from hell to heaven, from nothingness to God. The starting point: matter, destination: the soul. The hydra at the beginning, the angel at the end."

Performing is all about feelings, the feelings that you absorb through the characters and those that you project to the public. Performing in *Les Misérables* was a way for me to heal myself. It was all about finding the essence of life, which is the consummate love of family, love of people, love of community. I even committed to marrying Sara—a third marriage takes guts and love!

In the end, Jean Valjean redeems himself through his love of people and his community. As he dies, the spirit of Fantine guides him into heaven, reminding him that "to love another person is to see the face of God." His spirit joins the people of Paris to fight for justice and equality hoping for a new day starting....

> Do you hear the people sing?
> Lost in the valley of the night?
> It is a music of the people
> who are climbing to the light.
>
> . . .
>
> Do you hear the people sing
> do you hear the distant drums?
> It is the future that they bring
> When tomorrow comes
> Tomorrow comes!

Gino in Classic Concert with l'Orchestre Métropolitain de Montréal

Gino on his arrival in New York, 1967

Gino at age 16

Début at the Paris Opera in
l'Héritière, **1980**

As Figaro in Paris - Théâtre des
Champs-Élysées, 1983

In *Montségur,* **1986**

As Iago in Portland,
Oregon

With Maestro Steven Mercurio in concert in Italy

With Maestro Zubin Mehta at the Royal Opera House, London

With Barbara Hendricks before launch of
La Bohème **film**

**With Neil Shicoff at
Convent Garden**

With Marcello Mastroianni at Cinecittà, Rome

With Joan Baez, in San Francisco after Gino's performance of *Don Giovanni*

With Luciano Pavarotti in *La Bohème* – San Francisco Opera, 1988

With Cecilia Bartoli in *The Barber of Seville*, Dallas Opera, 1993

With Ben Luxon and Jon Vickers in *Peter Grimes* at the Paris Opera, 1981

With José Carreras in filming *La Bohème*, 1988

Gino and Mirella Freni in *La Bohème*, 1991

Gino and Louis in *Don Giovanni*, 1988

With Luciano Pavarotti in San Francisco after *La Bohème* performance

With Giuseppe di Stefano in Milan, before Gino's *La Bohème* debut

With Roberto Alagna in Paris after *Lucia di Lamermoor*

Gino with Marie-Josée Lord and Luc Plamondon

Gino As Quasimodo in *Notre Dame de Paris*

With trumpeter Vincenzo Guzzo at the LADISQ Gala at the nomination of *Serata D'Amore*

With Dominic Boulianne before recital in Saint-Pétronille, Quebec, 2014

Kathryn Stephenson

Kathryn, Le Sofia and Enrico

Enrico, Sofia and Gino

Gino as Jean Valjean in *Les Misérables*, With son Enrico in *The Barber of Seville*, Toulouse, 1989

With Sofia in Christmas concert in Vieux Montréal, Chapelle Notre-Dame-de-Bon-Secours, 2019

Lina, before her death, with Sofia and Enrico

Gino and wife his Sara

Gino as Jean Valjean in Les Misérables, *Les Misérables*, 2008

Gino's Emmy Award, 1995

Quilico Family IBM Award

Gino's Officer of the Order of Canada Award

Louis's Companion of the Order of Canada Award

FINALE
Summer 2020

In surreal images, 2020 has brought the world to its knees in more ways than one. Locked down and isolated in my condo with my wife, I watched the protests all over the world, with thousands of people of all races and colours, chanting, "I CAN'T BREATHE". At the same time, thousands of others have died struggling to do just that. That thousands of people have joined this chorus is an affirmation that love may still overcome hate, discrimination, and social inequality. The Coronavirus disease has further demonstrated that we're all human and vulnerable to the same laws of nature.

I felt the constant threat of the COVID-19 bug. With every slight cough and throat irritation, I feared I had caught virus. I never did, yet I imagined and feared the worst, while Sara had no symptoms or imaginary fears. Is this the way I'll go? I asked myself, at the tender age of sixty-five, the new forty-five, struggling for breath while waiting for an ambulance to take me to a hospital that is most likely overcrowded, understaffed, and under-equipped? Will I die under a ventilator, struggling for the breath that I have spent a life controlling? From morning till night, the television covered no news other than the statistics of COVID-infected seniors dying en masse around the world.

For the music and entertaining field, it felt like the end of the world. Would our industry ever rise again to its pre-COVID days? My concerts were all cancelled. People sang from balconies and found new ways to connect. The internet became our best friend by bringing virtual concerts and shows into our homes. Whether this proves a temporary fix or a new way of bringing music to the masses remains to be seen.

During the Christmas season, I played my recordings of *La Bohème*. The poverty, grief, and loss suffered by its characters seemed magnified by the pandemic, which, like a cancer, has inflicted great harm and a great sense of uncertainty on the music.

Thankfully, I also had my vast library of CDs to filter out the noise of broadcasters and end-of-days predictions. The music brought back memories, took my mind off any dark thoughts, and even controlled my fear of contracting the virus. When I felt something coming up, Chamomile and night-time Tylenol helped me go to sleep and float away from my body.

My father had been a very spiritual man, even believing he had once spoken directly to God. More than ever, he was in my thoughts and my dreams while isolated from the world. I tried to connect with him in spirit, and I often dreamt of him. I don't always remember my dreams, only the vague images and sensations with which they leave you on waking up.

In my recurrent dreams, I'm forever a small, skinny kid lost in a too-large palace of many rooms. In one of those dreams that stayed with me after waking, I'm in a museum. I run from one room to another, shaking from fright at the large paintings on the wall, depicting people killing each other, women cutting men's throats, images of crucified Christs, while throngs of people carry handmade signs that proclaim: No Justice, No Peace! I scream. A hunchbacked jester in full regalia and makeup takes me by the hand and sits me on his lap to cuddle me. I recognize him.

"Please forgive me," I say, "if I stopped speaking to you."

"Don't mention it," he says, "you're sitting on my lap, now. You're fine."

"Life took such a crazy turn after mother died," I say.

"What are you talking about? Your mother is next to me, practising next door."

I hear the familiar sound of a piano and try to run towards it, but he holds me tight, "Wait a minute before you go. Remember that life is bigger than all of us. It's a humongous wall. It gives back only what you throw at it.... But enough sermons, for now, let's go join your mother."

I run through a dark void, feeling choked. "I'm afraid of losing my breath," I cry. The tunnel gets lighter and lighter the higher I fly, and finally, I'm in the next room, but it's not a room at all. There are no walls! It's full of light, and I see my mother smiling.

"Don't come close to me," I tell her, "I may be sick. Haven't you heard of the Coronavirus?"

"Haven't you heard that spirits are immune to any virus? Look above."

I see a translucent circle of light above us that has illuminated the room without walls.

"That's a Corona, too," she says. "It's made up of millions of particles of human breath that create a circle of light around the globe. Once you get the virus, you're part of the light and you become immune like me. Don't be afraid."

"But the injustices, the people, the rage. How will it all end?"

"What have I always told you? It will only end if you fight the dark with the light."

She points to an old-fashioned camera on a tripod. "Come Louis. Let's take a family photo, to remember the moment," she says.

The three of us pose for a photo. "Oh, yes," I laugh, "The father, the son and the holy spirit."

A light flashes and we bow, together again, forever.

Lina, Louis and Gino at the Maurice-Richard Arena, Montreal,1984
(photo-Guy Dubois)

Acknowledgements

This book would not have been possible without (that's a Gallicism) of Gino Quilico. He gave generously of his time to provide me with the details of his family's story, his reflections and observations on the opera world, and did not shy away from revealing his most personal feelings, fears, and joys. His passion for the roles that consumed most of his artistic life gave me the impetus to delve into the human emotions that erupt from opera stages and often carry over into the lives of the performers. I would also like to thank members of his family that agreed to be interviewed: David Quilico, Madeleine Quilico, Kathryn Stephenson, Sara Decayette.

I wish to acknowledge Ruby Mercer's book, *The Quilicos, Louis, Gino & Lina: An Operatic Family* (Toronto: Mosaic Press, 1991), which has been a source of essential background information.

A big *merci* goes to Athala Bissonnette who offered to translate the English text into French in a timely and efficient manner and made it possible for the French version to be published simultaneously with the original. I was thrilled when both books found their rightful home thanks to the enthusiastic reception of Linda Leith Publishing. Many heartfelt thanks go to Linda Leith and her associate publisher, Leila Marshy, for their help.

I am forever grateful to my writing group colleagues, Susan Doherty, Josée Lafrenière, Gina Roitman, and Liz Ulin, who offered, through

Zoom meetings, valuable and encouragement during the most isolating pandemic period.

And thank you to my wonderful sons and their families, who provide the love and support we all need when pursuing elusive artistic goals.